# COPING WITH DEPRESSION IN THE MINISTRY AND OTHER HELPING PROFESSIONS

Also by Archibald D. Hart, Ph.D.

*Feeling Free*

*Depression: Coping and Caring*

*Children and Divorce: What to Expect, How to Help*

*The Success Factor: Discovering God's Potential
through Reality Thinking*

# COPING WITH DEPRESSION IN THE MINISTRY AND OTHER HELPING PROFESSIONS

## ARCHIBALD D. HART, Ph.D.

**WORD BOOKS**
PUBLISHER
WACO, TEXAS

A DIVISION OF
WORD, INCORPORATED

COPING WITH DEPRESSION IN THE MINISTRY
AND OTHER HELPING PROFESSIONS

Unless otherwise marked, all Scripture quotations are from the
King James Version of the Bible.

Quotation marked NEB is from The New English Bible, copyright
The Delegates of the Oxford University Press and The Syndics of the Cambridge
University Press, 1961, 1970.

Quotation marked NIV is from the New International Version of the Bible,
copyright © 1978 by New York International Bible Society.

Library of Congress Cataloging in Publication Data:

Hart, Archibald D.
    Coping with depression in the ministry and other helping professions.

    1. Clergy—psychology.   2. Depression, Mental.
I. Title.
BV4398.H37     1984     253'.2     84-3558
ISBN 0-8499-0365-3

*Printed in the United States of America*

To all the pastors,
missionaries, and Christian workers
who have provided the clinical experience behind this book.

Also, to Dr. Carl Tracie,
whose encouragement and friendship gave birth to the idea
that this book should be written.

# CONTENTS

List of Figures   ix

Preface   xi

A Note to Women Readers   xv

1. Depression in the Twentieth Century   1

2. The Emotional Hazards of Ministry   12

3. Spiritual Causes and Consequences of Psychological
Depression   24

4. The Many Faces of Depression   33

5. The Purposeful Nature of Depression   46

6. The Concept of Loss and the Depression Cycle   55

7. The Phases of Depression—Onset   65

8. The Phases of Depression—Middle Stage   74

9. The Phases of Depression—Recovery   87

10. The Professional Treatment of Depression   97

11. Why Ministers Burn Out   113

12. Depression in the Minister's Family   128

13. Building Resistance to Depression   143

Conclusion   155

# LIST OF FIGURES

1. The Sequence of Events in the Perception of Loss   42

2. A Model for Understanding Loss   56

3. The "Ideal" Depression Cycle   60

4. The "Typical" Depression Cycle   61

5. The Self-Perpetuating Depression Spiral   62

6. The Phases of Reactive Depression   66

7. Emotional Chaining   70

# PREFACE

For many years I have been particularly concerned about ministers and others who are called into Christian service. Shortly after my conversion at the age of eighteen, I became a lay preacher, and for a time I believed God was calling me to be a minister. In fact, my wife often jokes that when we married she believed she was getting a preacher! But it did not seem that this was in God's plan for my life, and so I began my first career as a civil engineer.

When I was twenty-four, however, God did allow me an experience which in many ways laid the foundation for much of what I am doing now. He allowed me to serve as a lay pastor to a small, low-income community on the outskirts of the city in South Africa where I lived and practiced engineering. I would conduct the Sunday school and preach the evening service, and my wife and I would visit and attempt to evangelize the people of this community. This arrangement continued for just over four years, during which I experienced something of what it was like to be a pastor. It was out of this experience that my need to know more about people and to learn how to help them with their problems grew. Eventually I turned to clinical psychology as my ministry.

As I became known as a competent psychologist who was also a Christian and who desired to integrate theology with my clinical skills, ministers and other Christians in helping professions began to see me about their problems. It has been my privilege, both in South Africa and in the eleven years I have been in the United States, to work with many of these people in a clinical setting. Out of this experience I have developed courses which I teach at our seminary to both emerging and experienced ministers.

I believe God has used my experience as a lay pastor, my extensive clinical work with ministers and other Christian workers, and the courses I teach to give me a special understanding of the problems of the ministry and other helping professions—an understanding which I feel compelled to communicate. (While the focus of this book will be primarily on preachers and pastors, I hope much of it will be helpful to counselors, teachers, missionaries, and others as well.)

In my opinion, the average seminary does not put enough emphasis on helping prospective ministers and Christian workers develop the emotional and interpersonal skills they will need in their work. Often ministers can preach captivating sermons, but they cannot handle their own anger constructively. They can teach theology but are hopelessly inadequate at resolving conflicts. They can pray for the gospel to reach every corner of the world and motivate others to do the same, only to find that it has bypassed their own children. There is more to being a Christian worker than being able to preach, pray, and understand the Scriptures. The *person* of the worker is as important as the skills and knowledge he or she possesses, and it is the preparation of the person that is often the most neglected in seminary and graduate-school training.

Nowhere is this lack of adequate preparation more devastating in its consequences than in the area of depression. And it is easy for ministers and other people helpers to become depressed, although such depression is often unacknowledged or misunderstood. In fact, it has been my experience in working with many ministers, Christian workers, and their families that not only is depression the most common emotional problem, but it is also the most destructive, both for the person who experiences it and for the many who look to him or her for spiritual guidance. I have come to believe that this high incidence of depression is no coincidence—that it is directly related to the nature of ministry and Christian service. It can even be called a vocational hazard!

There are many reasons why depression is so common in the ministry, and I will be attempting to develop an understanding of these in this book. My analysis will be focused primarily on the nature of the work and how it affects the minister as a person. Of course, it is also appropriate to ask about the spiritual dimensions of this problem. Sin and confused priorities contribute to the problems of the minister, just as they do with any person. But my reason for focusing on the vocational aspect in this book is simply that it has been the most neglected.

It is very easy to be so caught up in the spiritual implications of what one does that one forgets that the work must be accomplished through a human body—with human hands, a human mind—and in the context of other human beings. Because the problems that develop are psychological in nature, and therefore not readily measured or seen, there is a tendency to look only for spiritual reasons. The more obvious human factors can elude recognition and acknowledgment.

Ministers, like all people, are subject to natural laws which operate according to well-understood psychological principles. When these laws are abused, certain natural consequences can prevent God's Spirit from working effectively through his human agent. While I know that many spiritual components operate in ministry and that God can, and does, overrule human limitations at times, my goal in this book is to communicate where, when, and under what conditions the effectiveness of ministry may be undermined by the obvious, natural, and inevitable consequences of the abuse of mind and body. This emphasis, I hope, will restore balance to our understanding *without* undervaluing the spiritual components. Indeed, these spiritual components can be channeled more constructively towards the healing of our total persons if we have a better understanding of how our bodies and minds operate. This is especially true in the area of depression.

Nothing I say in this book is intended to detract from the power of God to heal our broken minds and disturbed emotions. The Holy Spirit *is* the great healer and his work in the lives of ministers and of all people must be allowed to take preeminence. My concern is that ignorance of simple psychological and physiological laws can *obstruct* the work of the Holy Spirit. It is almost as if Satan, unable to obstruct God's Spirit directly, has encouraged the development of erroneous beliefs and irrational thought processes so as to create havoc in otherwise spiritually sound individuals.

A distorted belief about the nature and function of depression can produce consequences more serious than those of depression itself. I call this a "bondage of misunderstanding." Through such misunderstanding, Christian workers can become incapacitated. Brilliant and dedicated ministers can become ineffectual.

If you suffer from depression, or have done so in the past, I trust that what follows will help you to unlock your prison of misunderstanding and experience healing. If you have not yet experienced depression, then I hope that what I have to say will help to prevent such an experience and will help you understand depression when it happens to others. It is my prayer that a better understanding of the nature and purpose of depression will open the way for the Holy Spirit to bring healing to those who are:

. . . as workers together with him. . . . Giving no offence in any thing, that the ministry be not blamed: But in all things approving ourselves as the ministers of God, in much patience, in afflictions, in necessities, in distresses (2 Cor. 6:1–4).

ARCHIBALD D. HART, PH.D.
Pasadena, California

# A NOTE TO WOMEN READERS

Any use of the masculine pronoun in this book is not intended to be sexist. While most ministers are currently male, and much of my experience in counseling with ministers and their families has been with the typical male minister, many denominations are now ordaining women. A fair number of husband-and-wife ministerial teams are also emerging. These are exciting developments and the next decade may well see a new focus in the problems and joys of ministry.

While ministry has been a male-dominated vocation, women have served the church as missionaries and educators for many decades. I have, therefore, sought to address the problems of depression in the helping professions from the perspective of both sexes. I have endeavored to use inclusive language wherever possible to show my respect for the important role women have played in Christian work. Where I do unavoidably use the pronoun "he," except in cases where the gender of the antecedent is clearly identified, I would ask my reader to use it in reference to either sex.

# COPING WITH DEPRESSION IN THE MINISTRY AND OTHER HELPING PROFESSIONS

# 1

## DEPRESSION IN THE TWENTIETH CENTURY

Peter had been a minister in a large Protestant denomination for about fifteen years. He was a dynamic preacher and had been extremely effective in two previous pastorates. One morning, about a year after he had begun work in his present pastorate, he awoke to find himself obsessed with thoughts of death. He could not shake these thoughts; the more he tried to stop them, the more they seemed to haunt him. He was barely able to drag himself out of bed in the mornings; a great heaviness seemed to hold him down. He moved slowly and with great effort and could hardly finish shaving and brushing his teeth. Many mornings he found himself heading back to his bed, where he sometimes remained for days. During the daytime he just wanted to sleep. At night he would toss restlessly, obsessed with fears that he would never be able to sleep again.

Peter's wife was alarmed. What was happening? What could she do to shake Peter out of this strange behavior? At last, moved by sheer desperation, she called me.

Peter was experiencing what millions of Americans will experience at some time in their lives: depression.

Of course, it doesn't always strike in quite the same way. Some are only slightly affected while others are completely immobilized by it. Any of these symptoms may be present:

—confused thinking,
—inability to reason or make decisions,
—slowed speech,
—loss of interest in work or hobbies,
—inertia,
—fear of losing one's mind,
—flogging oneself with guilt and self-reproach,

—thoughts of death and death wishes,
—feelings of hopelessness and inadequacy,
—inability to concentrate,
—loss of appetite or a marked increase in appetite,
—feeling of total futility,
—inability to sleep or oversleeping,
—stomach discomfort.

Sometimes the depression hits like a bolt of lightning. Sometimes it creeps up like a cat stalking a bird—slowly and insidiously. Often the sufferers can give no clear reason why they feel as they do. They certainly cannot shake off the feelings. The depression may last a few days or it may last for years.

When I first saw Peter, he could not explain why he felt the way he did. His home life was good. His wife was a patient and loving person and his children were well behaved. His work as the senior pastor of a large congregation was satisfying. Though he admitted that there were some conflicts brewing in his church he did not see these as threatening or upsetting. "Nothing is wrong with my life so far as I can see," he insisted.

But as I began to explore his feelings and thoughts we agreed that his garden wasn't full of roses. The weeds of self-doubt emerged. His self-confidence was waning. Many influential members of his congregation were beginning to resist his ideas and give him a hard time at committee meetings. It was very clear that Peter was experiencing a significant loss in his vocational effectiveness. Even though he was not able to identify his many conflicts and could not consciously admit what was happening, his body system was responding with the normal, natural, and expected response—it became depressed.

Ideally, depression performs a very important function. It triggers a series of important responses in the body to deal with the chaos in life. Peter's depression was forcing him to withdraw from his troublesome environment so that he could regain his perspective and make appropriate adjustments. As we will see later, this purposeful function of depression is frequently overlooked by lay people as well as psychologists. I believe it provides the key to unlocking the misery and mystery of this affliction.

## Depression in History

Depression has afflicted humanity since creation. In fact, remarkably accurate descriptions have come down to us from ancient times. Hippocrates and Galen in their writings both stressed the existence of the depressive mood. The early Greek, Roman, and Arab physicians knew that retarded thinking, slowed speech, and sluggish movements were obvious features of the depressed condition.

Of course, treatment in those early days followed the then-accepted theory of the causes of depression. Since many believed that a "noxious humor" and disharmony of the "normal" body humors was at fault, bleeding, purgation, and sweating were commonly employed as efforts to restore the "harmony." Fortunately, this early method of treatment often also included nutritious food, satisfactory fluid intake, ensuring regular bowel movements, sufficient sleep, and a balance of rest and exercise, as well as the removal of "disturbing influences," so that a remarkable and very effective cure was often achieved for these early sufferers. It is not surprising, therefore, to find that these early therapeutic practices, with some variations, were followed by the physicians of the Western world up into the sixteenth and seventeenth centuries.

It was not until the seventeenth century that further clinical progress in observation and understanding of the depressive illness was made. In that century, as a result of progress in chemistry, anatomy, and the general understanding of emotional disorders, there emerged a variety of newer theories. By the eighteenth century the relationship of emotion to the somatic or bodily system was becoming clearer. In the nineteenth century the fact that depression could occur either as an isolated illness or as a periodic problem (sometimes alternating with times of manic excitement) was generally accepted.

During the past twenty years, interest in the problem of depression has risen sharply. Impetus has come from the introduction of antidepressant medication and, more recently, a simple test for the efficacy of treatment by medication for some forms of depression. These developments have underscored the probability that biochemical and physiological factors contribute greatly to the origin of much severe depression. Effective diagnostic tools will soon help the clinician distinguish between depressions which may be primarily physiological in nature and those which are psychological.

Despite these advances, depression is still poorly understood. Too many clinicians still hold tenaciously to their individual and outdated theories. The age-old mind-body dilemma is still very much with us. The link between the body and the mind remains a mystery.

## The Many Faces of Depression

We now know that depression affects people of different age groups differently. The fact that depression may present radically different symptoms confuses the picture even more. The depression of an ado-

3

lescent whose physiology is undergoing rapid change may reveal itself quite differently from the depression of an elderly person whose brain functions are showing marked signs of deterioration. Yet we still label both as "depression." The depression of a sophisticated socialite having problems with her eldest son may show itself quite differently than the depression of the primitive African who believes his ancestral spirits are displeased with him. Making sense of the common denominator, depression, is therefore no easy task.

All this is to say that depression is a complex emotion, not always recognizable by the depressed individual. It may express itself in many guises and may or may not be a consequence of what is happening in the environment. Therefore, the minister or Christian worker who adopts a simplistic, single-cause theory about his depression or who does not readily recognize his emotional discomfort as depression only increases the misery of the experience. Spiritualizing a problem which is psychological or physiological in nature may hinder attempts to get at the real cause of the problem (just as psychologizing a spiritual problem may hinder spiritual healing). My goal in this book is to help the reader make discriminating judgments about the cause of a particular depression and thus begin to find a way out of it. The misunderstanding of depression, especially the error of attributing it to the wrong cause, is the single most influential factor that perpetuates a depression beyond the point of early recovery.

## Depression—the Dominating Emotion of Our Age

While depression has existed from the beginning of time, our present age is seeing a marked increase in the incidence of low-grade, persistent depression in the Western world. While the incidence of severe psychotic depression is about the same worldwide (it appears to be a function of genetic factors) the prevalence of the lesser debilitating depressions differs widely from culture to culture.

A culture such as ours, where there is a high priority placed on performance and success as symbols of worthiness and where there is a diminishing opportunity to be successful, is bound to give rise to an increased gap between expectations and accomplishments. This in turn creates disillusionment, the apparent loss of a dream. And the vocation of ministry is not exempt from this loss.

Many psychological and sociological commentators have made reference to this prevalent sense of loss. They emphasize there is now very clear evidence that the "age of anxiety" that characterized the first half of this century has given way to an "age of melancholia"—that depression is the dominant mood of our age. Mental health statistics appear to support this interpretation. The suicide rate has increased dramatically over the past twenty years. Women are now higher on the suicide-risk scale, and the median age for suicide is now just under thirty—and dropping. Both are significant changes. Before World War I, the median suicide age was between forty and fifty and men were at greater risk.

But societal disillusionment is not the only factor contributing to the rise of depression in our age. Equally important is the increasing abuse and misuse of the body. *Stress* is the key word explaining this abuse. The more complex a culture, the greater is the experience of stress. The consequent physiological distress plays havoc with the biochemical processes of the body, and depression is a symptom and the natural outcome of this distress. Who would disagree that the pace of our Western lifestyle is less than ideal? The intensity of our work and living is placing demands on our physiology for which it was not designed. In previous ages, the time it took to get from one place to another provided our biological system with ample opportunity to rest, recover, and restore its balance. Our speeded-up world no longer provides this for us; the time we save traveling speedily to work or to another city is used for additional work activity instead of stress recovery. This is the trap of technological efficiency—the time we save by doing something quickly is given to doing something else! The result has been a marked increase in the incidence and severity of stress-related disorders, including depression.

Perhaps a personal example would be helpful. I recently spoke to a large church gathering in the East. The two-day speaking assignment required me to travel two thousand miles, and this distance could be flown in about four hours. If I had traveled by train it would have taken me, I suppose, about six days total, leaving me with three days' rest time. But I was a victim of my efficiency. The travel time itself did not provide rest—it was too short. I planned my trip so as to return from the East late on a Saturday evening in time to be up early on Sunday to fulfill a speaking engagement in Los Angeles. Naturally, the following week I paid for my hectic schedule in depression, fatigue, and loss of efficiency in the tasks I tried to perform. I should have planned for recovery time.

While a few such abuses do not have serious and long-term effects, repeatedly subjecting our bodies to this kind of stress will take its toll. It takes courage, determination, and a clear awareness of how stress produces depression to avoid these traps. We have only ourselves to blame if we become trapped by our twentieth-century efficiency!

## How Common Is Depression?

Depression is a lot more common than the average person realizes. Sufferers from depression often feel they are the only people ever to have suffered like this; they take it very personally. But the ability to suffer depression is the lot of all humankind; we are built to experience it.

Every person experiences the repeated cycles of being in and out of a "normal" depression. Sadness, discouragement, pessimism, and a sense of hopelessness must surely overtake all of us from time to time. These are called "reactive" depressions. I occasionally hear someone say, "But I honestly never feel depressed." Is it possible to be completely free of these normal depressions? I doubt it! Those who claim never to be depressed are probably not using the correct label for the emotion. They misunderstand what depression really is—either they do not readily recognize the symptoms of depression, or they simply have another label for it.

These "normal" depressions, while being unpleasant and even noxious, are mostly short-lived and self-limiting. When they pass, we incorporate them into our experience and move on with a new perspective.

Sometimes these depressions don't pass so readily. In various ways, which I will discuss later, we perpetuate and even intensify what would otherwise be a normal depression. A prolonged experience of a deep depression then ensues. Thus a normal depression becomes "abnormal" by virtue of the fact that it has moved from being purposeful to becoming destructive.

## Abnormal Depressions

A group of depressive disorders always considered to be "abnormal" are those which are psychotic in nature. These depressions are so severe that the sufferer loses contact with reality, becomes delusional, and cannot take care of himself or herself. These psychotic depressions are considered by most authorities to have biochemical causes. Whether milder forms of these abnormal depressions (sometimes called "endogenous") are on a continuum with normal depression is uncertain, but I personally do not believe so. Psychotic depression clearly stands apart and is both qualitatively and quantitatively different from other depressions.

Statistically speaking, while normal depression is the experience of every person, about one in five will experience the symptomatology to even a moderate degree. Only one percent of the population suffers a psychotic depression.

While some depressions clearly are the consequence of physiological disturbances, mainly disturbances of biochemical systems, the environment will also play a determining part. Where there is stress, an unsatisfactory support system, work dissatisfaction, interpersonal conflict, marital unhappiness, and/or feelings of helplessness, the frequency and intensity of depression will be greater, no matter what the underlying cause of the depression. Environmental factors will operate to increase the tendency to depression as well as to reduce the resources needed to make appropriate adjustments to the depressing event.

Unfortunately, this diminished capacity to tolerate depression is present to a marked degree in the vocation of ministry and many of the helping and teaching professions.

## Depression in Biblical Context

The term depression is not used in the Bible. It is a technical term of more recent origin. Very accurate descriptions of depression are nevertheless to be found in Scripture. Biblical terms such as *despair, cast down, sad,* and *sighing* all refer to forms of the depressive syndrome.

It is also very common for a biblical character to express a desire that God would take his life. For example, in Numbers 11:15, Moses prays: "And if thou deal thus with me, kill me, I pray thee, out of hand, if I have found favour in thy sight; and let me not see my wretchedness."

Elijah prayed a similar prayer during his depression (1 Kings 19:4), and Job expressed his death wish clearly when he cursed the day of his birth and said: "Wherefore is light given to him that is in misery, and life unto the bitter in soul; Which long for death, but it cometh not; and dig for it more than for hid treasures" (Job 3:20-21).

Loss of appetite as a symptom of depression is seen in the story of Ahab, who couldn't get Naboth's vineyard (1 Kings 21:4); in Hannah, whose womb the Lord had shut up (1 Sam. 1:7); and in Saul, who had just heard the prophecy of Samuel that Israel would be delivered into the hands of the Philistines (1 Sam. 28:23).

The Psalms are full of references to depression and consequently have been a major source of comfort to the despairing and downcast. Jesus himself, while praying in the Garden of Gethsemane, "began to be sorrowful and very heavy" (Matt. 26:37).

My purpose in drawing attention to these obvious references to depression in Scripture is to emphasize that depression has always been a part of human experience and that it is a natural and normal response to a particular set of circumstances.

## Erroneous Christian Ideas about Depression

Frequently I encounter devout Christians, including ministers, who cannot accept the fact that depression is a normal part of human experience. Their refusal to accept it as such is equivalent to refusing to accept that pain is an inevitable part of human existence. Designed as we are to experience physical pain, we readily accept its purposeful function as a warning system alerting us to impending disaster or disease and forcing us to take corrective healing steps. Depression, in many of its forms, has an identical purpose. Its intended function is to warn us that something is wrong and needs attention. The symptoms of depression have the purpose of forcing us to retreat from our environment so that we can have an opportunity to deal with the cause, or at least cope with it. Sometimes the cause is physical, and the depression slows us down so that we may more rapidly recover from the illness. Sometimes the cause is psychological, and the depression should be used as an opportunity to make appropriate adjustments in the way we think or relate to other people.

Depression is always purposeful. It is most unfortunate that, despite our sophisticated understanding of many human problems, we have lost sight of this normalizing function of depression.

More specifically, popular Christian thought involves a number of erroneous ideas about depression. These beliefs influence behavior and emotions, so I want to discuss a few of them briefly.

(1) *"All my depression comes from Satan."* Such an idea is based on the notion that depression is alien to the body and comes upon it as an outside force or intruder. The danger in this idea is that it puts the blame on the external force (Satan) and keeps us from facing the adjustments that are needed. It also leads to the idea that depression is evil. While satanic forces may operate to tempt us, with depression resulting when we succumb, the depression itself is not evil—any more than pain is evil. The depression is a normal and natural consequence.

(2) *"Depression is the consequence of my sin."* This idea is misleading because it implies that depression is the consequence of being unspiritual or unbelieving. "If you are depressed, then look for the sin that is causing the depression" is frequently the well-meant advice of uninformed pastors.

This idea fails to allow for the many times when the depression is a response to neutral events in which no good or bad issues are at stake. If I accidentally drop and break a cherished vase which belonged to my grandmother and which she lovingly entrusted to me before she died, I will experience a deep sadness. This sadness is a reactive depression and has nothing to do with sin. If a pastor is feeling sick but decides

8

nevertheless to preach, and if as a consequence of illness he or she does a poor job and feels bad about it afterwards, that depression also has nothing to do with sin. It is merely a natural consequence of certain unfortunate events.

(3) *"Depression is God punishing me."* It is important not to confuse *punishment* with *discipline*. Punishment is a "getting even," while discipline is intended to correct behavior. It is unfortunate that Christians have difficulty accepting the fact that God has provided forgiveness through the death of his Son, Jesus Christ, and the shedding of his blood. Either I am punished or I am forgiven. If I am punished I don't need forgiveness.

I have, unfortunately, heard a devout father say, "The reason my daughter has leukemia is that God is punishing me for what I have done behind my wife's back." Such a statement is "guilt talk." Why would God make someone else to suffer for his sin when Christ has already done all the suffering? No, these notions are erroneous. Depression may sometimes be the natural consequence of sin. And God may convict us of sin through depression, or he may use it as a message to get our attention or teach a better way to live. But this is not the same as seeing it as a form of punishment for sin. Depression must not be seen as God's punishment of one of his children—not since the Cross.

(4) *"Depression is not the will of God."* I suppose that in an idealistic sense we would be better off if we never became depressed. We would also prefer never to experience pain! But then how would we know when something was wrong with our bodies? As we have already seen, depression often fulfills a useful purpose. Besides, some depressions are the consequence of fatigue, viral infection, physical disease, and disturbances of hormonal and complex biochemical balances. Since God has created us, how can it not be within his will for us to experience these probelms that stem directly from the way we are made?

There are other erroneous ideas that are variations on the theme mentioned above: "Depression is a sign that you are not right with God"; "You should never be depressed if you are a Christian"; "Prayer can take away all depression"; and so on. All are misleading because they oversimplify the concept of depression, don't allow that depression is a normal process, and create unrealistic expectations and self-rejection in the minds of those who suffer depression. However, there is a form of depression that we could call "spiritual depression," and to which some of these statements may apply. I will discuss this in a later chapter.

## Should Christians Be Free of Depression?

One minister, whose depression had taken him very close to suicide as a means of relieving the intense misery he and his family were suffering, wrote to me:

In those black and bleak days when I was at my lowest, I was convinced God had abandoned me. "How could anyone who was a friend of God be so abandoned by him?" I asked myself. I became convinced that my depression was a sign that God had rejected me.

Such distorted feelings and thoughts are very common when we are depressed. Depression wreaks havoc on our perceptions and creates irrational beliefs. We desperately search for reasons to explain our depression. The search is very selective, as the depression itself causes us to attend only to the negative aspects of our lives.

Depression works like a pair of sunglasses; it causes everything to appear darker than it really is. Such was the experience of Elijah (1 Kings 19:4) when, after the victory over the prophets of Baal on Mount Carmel, he fled fatigued and depressed into the wilderness. There, under the juniper tree, things looked so bad he asked God to let him die. Two days of sleep and food from God's angels removed the depression so that he could go "in the strength of that meat forty days and forty nights" (v. 8).

The answer to the question, "Should Christians be free of depression?" becomes clearer when we ask another question: "Why should Christians be free of depression?" What special privilege does a Christian have to be exempt from the normal functions of the body? The answer is "none."

While I firmly believe that the committed Christian has tremendous *resources* for dealing wih the *causes* of depression, I see no evidence in Scripture to support the idea that, in the acceptance of the Christian faith and the accompanying new-birth experience, we are given a "go to heaven and bypass all human suffering" card. Yet this irrational and unconscious belief is very prevalent.

The problem exists because we do not understand the role of the emotions, especially the negative emotions, in the spiritual life of the believer. We accept physical pain and disease as a normal part of human existence, even though we may pray for healing. When the pain is emotional, however, we do not accept it in quite the same way. We question whether or not it should be present and do not readily accept the legitimacy of emotional pain.

All I have said thus far is not intended to deny that there are some aspects of depression, or more correctly, some *causes* of depression, which could be avoided if we sincerely believed the gospel and followed its teachings with full reliance upon God. I am convinced that the values of the Christian faith, the perspective that the claims of Christ presents, and the resources of prayer and Scripture can remove many causes of depression in the individual Christian believer. To be able to separate the essentials of life (as God presents them to us) from the nonessentials can so create a balance in our beliefs and attitudes that many of the conflicts and losses we experience could be reduced. Our experience of reactive depression would then dramatically decline. In other words, it is possible to avoid some depression if we stay close to God.

The reader will notice that I draw a distinction between the *causes* of depression and the *experience* of depression. The *experience* of depression is always legitimate. It is a natural and normal response to something happening either in our environment or in our bodies. The *cause* of depression may not be. We may be depressed over something that ought not to be depressing us. For example, if we are angry at ourselves because of a lost opportunity to make some money through a shady deal, the depression following the loss is a normal and legitimate response. However, if our moral sensibilities were firmly grounded in the righteousness of the gospel, we would not have valued the dishonest opportunity in the first place, and would not be depressed after losing it. The key to coping with depression, therefore, lies in removing the *cause* of the depression but not in fighting the *experience* of the depression itself. When the cause cannot be removed—as in, say, bereavement—the normal thing to do is grieve. In the final analysis, grieving is what most psychological depressions are all about, and Christians ought to know how to grieve—they have been given the resources for it!

# 2

## THE EMOTIONAL HAZARDS OF MINISTRY

Contrary to what many laypersons believe, depression is a major occupational hazard for ministers. For many ministers, surviving the ministry is a matter of surviving depression. Mostly the depression is not a positive experience. It robs the minister of power and effectiveness and destroys the joy of service.

It is impossible for anyone who has never been a minister to understand the loneliness, despair, and emotional pain that a large number of ministers must bear. Not a few leave the ministry altogether because of the debilitation of depression. Others exist in their pastorates in an unhappy, dissatisfied, and disillusioned state rather than leave their churches or change vocations.

In a report by the *Chicago Tribune* on 30 November 1980, the director of the Adult Chemical Dependency Treatment Unit at St. Mary's Hospital in Minneapolis, Minnesota, said, "Doctors, lawyers, and clergymen have the most problems with drug abuse, alcoholism, and suicide." It is not surprising to hear how vulnerable doctors and lawyers are to these problems, but the inclusion of clergymen in the list is sobering and shocking to many of us. The hidden problem behind the drug abuse, alcoholism, or suicide is very often depression, and these tragedies may merely serve to mask the real underlying problem.

I concede that since no specific details are given regarding the backgrounds and denominational affiliation of the ministers cited in this report, no definite conclusions can be drawn. I tend to doubt whether many of the alcoholic ministers were from evangelical denominations; however, from my experience in working with many ministers I can categorically say that equivalents of this problem *do* exist among evangelical pastors. The vocation of ministry is far from being a haven from the stresses of life. Among ministers and other helping professionals, the phenomenon of "burnout" is very common, and the disorders associated with too much stress, including the emotional problems of anxiety and depression, are all too frequently encountered in ministers by clinicians such as myself.

But let me hasten to add at this point, lest you consider me to be too harsh and critical, that there are also many happy and successful pastors. The work has many compensations, and the spiritual rewards of Christian service are very satisfying. My concern is that too many pastors never achieve this level of satisfaction, and we need to be honest enough in our evaluation to confront the real reasons for this.

## The Exacting Demands of Ministry

There is probably no other vocation in which it is possible to get away with as little hard work as in the ministry. Pastoral ranks have their share of lazy, incompetent, and ineffective workers, as do all vocations. But most ministers are conscientious and trustworthy and the majority have a tendency to be compulsive workers. Whether they start out this way or whether the vocation turns them into workaholics is not always clear. It is possible that the nature of the work attracts a responsive and conscientious type of person with high ideals and a strong need to serve others.

What then makes ministry so demanding—the conscientiousness of the minister or the nature of the work? I think both, so let us examine the characteristics of the worker and of the work so that you may better understand why ministers are especially vulnerable to depression.

First, the work demands a high level of internal control. Unlike other forms of employment in which supervisors, directors, managers, and the like provide an external system of direction, accountability, and control, ministers are "on their own." This encourages a heightened sense of responsibility. The pastor must utilize characteristics of conscientiousness, honesty, and accountability to God to do his work; and, while these internal control mechanisms are sometimes effective in producing high levels of work output, they can also be more demanding and exacting than external controls. It is easy to become perfectionistic when you are your own boss. As a consequence, the faithful, efficient minister in charge of a church often works harder and more conscientiously than most professionals in other occupations.

Not only does the average minister work harder, but he or she often struggles to live up to unrealistic, self-imposed expectations. Ministers often feel the need to be almost superhuman, possessing unusual gifts of intellect, social grace, and moral strength. They must be the perfect example of all the attributes of the Christian gospel. This is clearly an impossible situation, but many find themselves caught up in an endless cycle of attempting—and failing—to live up to these demands.

## The First Five Years

The seeds for problems in later ministerial life are usually planted during the first five years of service. It is during these years that habits and styles of operating are formed. In the beginning, fresh from seminary, pastors tend to look upon the work idealistically. They honestly believe they can solve any and all problems they will confront. But this cocksureness falters a little with the first experience of failure, and the trial-and-error learning which follows will either teach better coping skills or lay the foundation for future patterns of inadequate coping. As the years pass, these habitual and automatic patterns of coping, either constructive or destructive, become deeply entrenched.

The fortunate pastor learns quickly from both successes and failures and develops confidence in his or her own ability. He or she becomes more positive about the power of God in the ministry and develops a potent partnership with Christ. The unfortunate pastor also learns, but he or she learns less adequate responses. And, even though these do not work well, the pastor tends to retain them. Criticism destroys ambition, failing programs discourage hope, and the lack of spiritual vitality drains energy. The comprehensive and exacting demands of the Christian ministry take their toll. Such an individual, if he or she remains in the ministry, only goes through the motions of being a minister. Every day is drudgery and every sermon an unbearable rebuke. Depression becomes an increasingly common emotional state for such a pastor.

While the minister who has succumbed to the hazards of the vocation will experience a marked degree of depression, even the competent and fully functioning pastor is going to experience periods of despair and disappointment. One cannot succeed all the time. Some success may only serve to set a pastor up to expect more, and the disappointment may be greater when the next failure arrives.

The completely successful, never-make-a-mistake minister is a myth. He or she doesn't exist. Between the extremes of "completely successful" and "total failure" lies the majority of ministers. They have their successes, and they have their failures. While the ratio of successes to failures is high enough to keep them moving forward and persisting in their ministry, there are enough unrealistic expectations and insufficient resources to produce a state of frequent disappointment and despondency. Inevitably, the frequency of depressive reactions will

14

be especially high for ministers and those in similar helping professions.

## The Depression-Producing Hazards of the Ministry

Charles Hadden Spurgeon, the famous British preacher of the last century, became a minister at the age of eighteen. At twenty he went to London to serve as pastor of the New Park Street Chapel. His immediate popularity and the success of his preaching led to the erection of the huge Metropolitan Tabernacle in 1861, when he was only twenty-seven. Around this large church he developed a pastors' college at which he trained ministers. It continues to be a major training center for ministers from all around the world.

Among Spurgeon's many published lectures to his students is one entitled "The Minister's Fainting Fits." In this lecture Spurgeon, undoubtedly one of the greatest preachers who has ever lived, clearly identifies depression as a major vocational hazard for ministers. His statements are as true today as they were when presented to ministers a hundred years ago.

In the introduction to his lecture, Spurgeon says:

> As it is recorded that David, in the heat of battle, waxed faint, so may it be written of all the servants of the Lord. Fits of depression come over the most of us. Usually cheerful as we may be, we must at intervals be cast down. The strong are not always vigorous, the wise not always ready, the brave not always courageous, and the joyous not always happy.

Spurgeon himself was quick to admit that he was not immune to periodic bouts of depression. He said that he knew "by most painful experience what deep depression of spirit means, being visited therewith at seasons by no means few or far between." He then went on to cite from the biographies of Martin Luther and John Wesley, which are full of reports about their own experiences of depression. The experiences of depression, despair, and guilt led both these great men of faith to a fuller realization of God's provisions for ministry.

No doubt similar periods of depression in the lives of many devout and highly respected ministers of the gospel can be found. These examples suggest that depression is far more common among eminent ministers than is commonly supposed. Depression is no respecter of persons, and its presence does not deny the power of God or the earnestness of a pastor's commitment.

Drawing on Spurgeon's lecture and adding my own observations, I believe that the following factors are among those that contribute to the depression hazards of ministry:

(1) *Many ministers fail to take proper care of their bodies.* Depression is tied to our physiology as much as it is to our psychology. Even though in his day Spurgeon would have had a very limited understanding of the physiology of depression, he was remarkably accurate in identifying "certain bodily maladies, especially those connected with the digestive organs, the liver, and the spleen, as the 'fruitful foundations of despondency.'"

Spurgeon was also well aware that ministers often tend to neglect taking care of their physical needs. Quoting Burton's *Anatomy of Melancholy* and likening ministers to scholars in general, he said,

> Other men look to their tools; a painter will wash his pencils; a smith will look to his hammer, anvil, forge; . . . a musician will string and unstring his lute; only scholars (ministers) neglect that instrument (their brain and spirits, I mean) which they daily use. Well saith Lucan "See thou twist not the rope so hard that it break."

The fact that depression can sometimes be the result of disturbed physiology is an extension of the problem of being human. But the simple fact that depression may have physiological causes does not mean that this kind of depression is beyond voluntary control. There are many causes for physiological depression that can be avoided or controlled; for example, depressions that are the consequence of fatigue, stress, poor diet, or other abuse of the body. A person who knows or even suspects that he may have a thyroid or other endocrine problem should immediately see a doctor and take corrective steps to treat the problem. Neglecting to do this is sheer self-destruction. Allowing the continuation of suffering when modern medical science can provide relief and possibly a cure is irresponsible.

The minister who seldom or never engages in physical exercise is inviting the onset of depression. The work of ministry is sedentary in nature. It therefore takes deliberate planning and determined effort to make physical exercise a part of the daily routine. But studies have shown conclusively that the lack of adequate physical conditioning can have many disastrous consequences—both physical and psychological. In fact, a recent development in the treatment of severe depression is the use of vigorous exercise. The precise curative mechanism is not clearly understood, but the improvement in mood following adequate exercise is quite impressive.

(2) *The nature of the work produces depression.* The work of ministry, when it is undertaken with great sincerity and earnestness, is

bound to open the way to attacks of despondency. The weightiness of feeling responsible for the souls of others and of longing to see others experience the fullness of God's gift; the disappointment of seeing believers turn cold and pull away; the heartbreak of watching a married couple destroy each other, unable to utilize love and the grace of God in repairing their broken relationship—all will take their toll on sensitive and dedicated ministers.

Building God's church is, for many, a slow, laborious, sometimes glorious but often discouraging activity. This is not because the gospel is inadequate for modern day needs, but because humans are fickle, fearful, and fainthearted. If I throw a sharpened dart at a dartboard and it doesn't stick but falls to the ground, the problem is likely to be with the dartboard and not the dart! Its structure, like many cheap dartboards, lacks depth and resiliency and is therefore ineffective in receiving and holding the dart. Such is the case with so many people's hearts. All the same, it is difficult for a minister to watch the game of life as played by these people and not be pained by their weakness.

(3) *The minister's position in the church leads to loneliness.* Even the most well-equipped minister will not easily be understood by his congregation. "The most loving of his people cannot enter into his peculiar thoughts, cares, and temptations," Spurgeon says. The minister therefore usually finds himself standing above, beyond, and apart from his congregation.

A leadership role tends to set one apart no matter what the vocation. And a minister who is a true shepherd and servant of God, not just a hireling, will find this especially true. The pastor's life is marked by a type of loneliness which is peculiar to those who receive their calling from God. It is a solitude of sacredness, an isolation of the soul that feels the responsibility of eternal issues and must maintain its commitment to divine purposes above all else.

The kind of loneliness I am talking about does not come from physical isolation. It is felt even in crowded worship halls and intimate prayer groups. And it serves a purpose; it helps the pastor stand above the petty parochial interests of people who have too much investment in the here and now, and helps to keep the call and demands of the kingdom of God in the foreground.

Of course, such a loneliness does not, of itself, produce depression. It can, in fact, be an antidote for disillusionment and despair, since it provides a higher perspective against which the trivial experiences of ministry can be tested and disposed of. But so often I find that an unfortunate pastor has allowed this solitude to give way to a different type of isolation—the defensive, self-protecting false independence and stand-offishness of someone confused and out of control. Such a pastor is usually depressed, and often the depression goes unrecognized.

The loneliness of ministry, although essentially positive, can shape the minister toward being cut off from support systems. It can keep him from having close confidants with whom problems of the work can be discussed. It is a psychological fact that one cannot resolve conflicts or clarify issues simply by thinking about them. Self-talk and introspective rumination with no outside input leads inevitably to distortion and irrationality, whereas talking things over with someone else can help to clarify issues and remove distortions. Every minister needs close confidants—staff, family, other ministers, trusted laypersons in the congregation—to help in this clarifying process. If steps are not deliberately taken to develop these trusting and supportive relationships in each pastorate, the loneliness of leadership responsibility will lead to isolation and a distortion of reasoning—and this spells depression for many ministers.

(4) *Ministers tend not to know how to relax.* Work that occupies every waking moment for long periods of time—as the ministry often does—can lead to depression. Spurgeon says, "Repose is as needful to the mind as sleep to the body. Our Sabbaths are our days of toil, and if we do not rest upon some other day we shall break down. Even the earth must lie fallow and have her Sabbaths, and so must we."

Jesus also knew the importance of rest. You will recall how after John the Baptist had been beheaded and his disciples had buried him, the apostles, who were greatly distressed, gathered to tell Jesus what had happened: "And he said unto them, Come ye yourselves apart into a desert place, and rest a while" (Mark 6:31).

What? When people are dying and in need of help? When life is so short and there is so much to be done? Why did Jesus invite his disciples to rest awhile? Because he knew better than to fly in the face of the limitations of physical realities. The fact that Jesus could miraculously heal the sick did not give license for the abuse of his or anyone else's body and mind. Jesus knew better than to push himself and his followers to the point of exhaustion. His sensitivity to the needs of people was outstanding; it's a pity we cannot be as sensitive to our own needs.

Rest time is not wasted time! It is, in the long run, more economical and efficient to rest and gather fresh strength and perspective before going back to the battle. We know to rest a horse we've been riding or to cool an engine that's been overheating—but to rest ourselves seems so difficult.

One very common kind of depression in ministers is that which follows the performance of the ministerial duties on a Sunday. Sunday afternoons and Monday mornings bring a unique type of depression called the "postadrenalin blues." It is a purely physiological response, but often misunderstood and misinterpreted by the minister.

The scenario goes something like this: From the beginning of the week the focus is on the Sunday worship or evangelistic service. Sermon preparation, worship service design, hymn selection, visitation of newcomers, and so on—all have Sunday's activities as their goal and culmination. Subtle and often unrecognized anxiety pervades the anticipation of the weekend activity, and there is a gradual but steady buildup of adrenalin in the bloodstream. By the end of the week the minister is riding high on his excess of adrenalin. And then Sunday's activities are over, and there is a massive shutdown of the adrenal system. As a result, the minister is likely to experience a let-down feeling and a period of depression.

After any high level of activity, the endocrine system, which is designed primarily to deal with emergencies and threats, produces depression so as to demand time for recuperation. Depending on how extensive the activity and the depression, recovery may take anywhere from a few hours to a few days. In extreme cases where adrenalin exhaustion has taken place or when disease of the adrenal gland is present, recovery from a very stressful experience can take many months, during which time extreme fatigue and inability to handle even mild stress is felt.

These "postadrenalin" depressions are frequently misunderstood by pastors. The tendency is to spiritualize the problem and attribute the depression to false causes, and this in turn only compounds the misery of the experience. The best way to deal with these postadrenalin depressions is to allow ample time for rest and recuperation. The depression should not be interpreted as anything but a physiological reaction.

(5) *Distorted ideas about the nature of the ministry may contribute to depression.* Frequently, distorted ideas about what the vocation of ministry actually entails give rise to unreasonable expectations and hence depression. One common idea is that the ministry is a "sacred task" and a "high calling," and that it therefore demands a very unique sort of commitment. This idea is essentially true, but it can easily become twisted and set the pastor up for unreasonable expectations. When these expectations are not met, frustration and depression follow.

Most ministers believe that the work they are engaged in is the most important in all the world. Why do they believe this? Ideally, because in God's kingdom spiritual issues are paramount. But there are two widespread underlying ideas which are less valid and which may be quite damaging.

First, an exaggerated belief in the importance of the ministry can arise as a compensation for the many sacrifices ministers and their families must make in terms of time and money. Given comparable years spent in study and preparation, the minister is probably the lowest paid of all professionals and is, therefore, constantly made aware of what he is having to give up for the cause of his work. In this context, to compensate for the pain of the sacrifice, it is easy to exaggerate the importance of that work to the point of distortion.

Second, the belief that ministry is a superior line of work can be perpetuated by the common beliefs and stereotyping of lay people. Many church members, as well as those outside the church, perceive the ministry as "special" and "set apart." This idea, of course, is essentially true, but it can be distorted. Too often it is thought that, since the ministry is carried out as a service to God, the minister himself must be especially godlike. This tendency to deny the minister the right to be human can be very dangerous, especially when the minister himself begins to think that way.

In pointing out the distorted ideas about the ministry that may arise, I would never want to deny the importance of the ministry! There is an awesome responsibility attached to the care of souls. But I have found that those ministers who are especially effective both vocationally and spiritually do not dwell on the belief that the ministry is the greatest of all vocations. They tend to have a great sense of humility about the contribution they personally make and to stand in awe of what God does—with or without them. And, because they do not hold exaggerated expectations about their work, they are less likely to become depressed when their expectations are not met.

I once asked a surgeon friend who every day made decisions that could affect the life or death of a patient how he handled the responsibility of his work. His answer was most illuminating and, I think, absolutely correct and applicable to our discussion here. He replied, "You come to terms very early in your career with your fallibility. It's okay not to be perfect and to make mistakes!"

In my experience, a tendency toward depression in ministers (when it is not physiological) is directly related to an inability to accept fallibility. Such persons lack the courage to accept their imperfections! They cannot tolerate making mistakes. They must do everything perfectly. No minister can survive with such a tendency.

(6) *There are no clearly defined boundaries to the work.* The minister's task is immense. When is a day's work ever done? When can one relax with a sense of "Ah, I've completed what I set out to do today, so I am content!"? Even when a minister collapses exhausted into an easy chair at the end of a day, there is still a pervading sense of in-

completeness that keeps the body's systems in a state of alertness and makes full relaxation impossible.

The problem usually arises when a pastor is unable to "partialize" his work. Since the task seems formidable when taken as a whole, the only way to approach it is to break it down into smaller tasks that can be tackled one at a time. Because there is usually no clear "starting time" or "quitting time," each day's work needs to be assigned beforehand so that at the end of the day the pastor can experience a feeling of accomplishment. This technique is similar to what the compulsive runner must learn to do. To avoid overdoing and perhaps injuring himself, such an athlete must determine beforehand how far he will run, so that he will know when he is finished.

"Partializing" can be a very helpful way of putting boundaries on the day-to-day work of a minister. But many ministers make problems for themselves by taking the task of partializing to the other extreme—preparing impossibly long lists of tasks to be performed each day. Ministers who do this will find themselves feeling frustrated at the end of the day because of not being able to finish what they set out for themselves to do. It is essential that a realistic estimate be made of the tasks to be performed for the day. Otherwise the feeling of incompleteness accompanying an inability to complete a day's work can be a continuous source of depression.

(7) *The minister's focus can become too narrow.* Many aspects of ministry can cause a minister's life to become too narrow. The work can become totally consuming, the single purpose for living. The pastor thinks of little else, avoids all other interests, denies himself hobbies, and becomes so narrowly focused on his work that he loses a sense of balance. He will advocate that his congregation live well-balanced lives, but be blind to the distortions in his own life.

Such a singleness of purpose would be admirable if it did not produce disastrous consequences! The minister's family, in particular, suffers from the conflict of priorities that ensues. The spouse discovers that he or she cannot depend on the pastor's being available when promised, since the demands of work preempt previous commitments to the family. The typical story is: "I'm sorry, dear, but why don't you and the children go ahead without me? You see, this urgent matter has cropped up! . . ." And so the one-eyed monster creeps insidiously forward, devouring the happiness of those close to the minister—and all in the name of Christian service.

Unfortunately for the minister, this narrow focus also produces a high risk of depression. In the first place, it can exaggerate the other depression-producing factors we've looked at in this chapter—neglect of physical needs, the burden of responsibility for the souls of others,

21

loneliness and isolation, lack of relaxation and clearly defined boundaries, distorted ideas about the work. In addition, outside activities and relationships are important because they give the minister the perspective and the emotional outlets needed for dealing with the many frustrations that are inherent in the ministry.

This is not to say that the minister's work should not be important—or even central—in his or her life. Singleness of purpose is not necessarily a fault in a minister. But when it so distorts priorities that the minister neglects to care for his or her own person and give sufficient time to his or her family, singleness of purpose can lead to depression.

(8) *Ministers tend to confuse role identity with self-image.* I believe that one of the most important developmental tasks every minister must master is the task of separating his self-image from his role identity. There is a strong tendency for ministers to derive their self-image and thus their self-esteem from their vocational role. In other words, who they *are* is determined by what they *do*. Self-identity easily merges with role identity, so that it becomes increasingly difficult for ministers to separate themselves from their work and from the many roles they play as pastors.

This can create numerous problems for ministers. For one, their self-esteem, which is derived from their self-image, can become too closely tied to what they do. If they are successful in their work, they feel good about themselves. If they aren't successful, they feel bad about themselves. Unfortunately, though, whether pastors succeed or not is only moderately dependent upon the pastors themselves. Ministry is a team effort and involves many others (including laity support) for successful operation. Ministers who let their feelings about themselves depend on whether they are successful in their work are inviting depression. There must be a clear boundary between what the self *is* and what the self *does*, if one is to be mentally healthy.

Confusing self-image and role identity can be particularly devastating in its effect when the minister retires. A lifelong pattern of investing too much of the self in the work is difficult to reverse. Since so much of the self is tied up with work, not being able to continue working means a loss of the self, and a deep depression may follow.

Clearly, God did not intend that his ministers should be so attached to what they do. He wants us to derive our self-worth from the knowledge that we are his redeemed children, not from whether we are successful in our jobs. Confusing self-image and role identity only gets in the way of God's power to work through us in any vocational situation.

## Ministry in Perspective

Despite the hazards of ministry, the work of the pastor has many compensations. Our discussion would be incomplete without a brief reference to some of them. The joy of soul-winning, discipling, and building God's church knows no equal. Ministering to hurting, lonely, and frightened people is humbling but satisfying. No one can know more fully than the pastor the way people crave respect, sympathy, understanding, and acceptance, and this knowledge can serve as a great hedge against his or her own happiness. And who better than a pastor can experience the comfort of divine support, the renewal of spirit by a healing God who ministers to bruised and battered souls?

Who is better equipped to be undeterred by faithless people than one whose heartstrings have been touched by the Holy Spirit called by a divine summons to preach the gospel and minister to needy people? Who is better fortified for the lonely road of ministry than one who has been given the calm and convincing belief that he or she is not alone in this task, that he or she can utterly depend on resources from above for help in enduring the trials of service? These are the blessings that a minister knows, and most ministers will attest that these are more than adequate compensations for the many sacrifices that must be made.

# 3

## SPIRITUAL CAUSES AND CONSEQUENCES OF PSYCHOLOGICAL DEPRESSION

At this point, many of you, if you are at all like the ministers I see in therapy, will be asking the question: "But isn't depression a spiritual rather than a psychological problem?" or, "Even if depression is a psychological (or even a physical) problem, is it not caused primarily by spiritual factors?"

For the Christian these are important questions. In one sense, *all* problems are spiritual. But questions like those posed above are more specific and cannot be satisfactorily answered by a general statement. Since the spiritual life of a believer is bound to be a central factor in his or her life, there may certainly be spiritual implications in a believer's depression. But how does one tell when a depression is purely spiritual, when it has some spiritual components, or when it is totally unrelated to spiritual issues? You may have read a book by Dr. Martyn Lloyd-Jones called *Spiritual Depression: Its Causes and Cure* (Grand Rapids, Mich.: Wlm. B. Eerdmans, 1965). While it is an excellent book, and I highly recommend it for general reading, it does create in some people's minds the impression that *all* depression is spiritual. This leads to confusion and may cause Christians who experience depression to engage in unnecessary spiritual self-punishment.

Dr. Lloyd-Jones did not intend this confusion. Before he became a minister he was a medical doctor, so he understands very well the differences between various forms of depression. I believe a more accurate title for his book would be *Spiritual Discontent*. Clearly, discontent is the cause of much unhappiness, but there are many important differences between discontent and psychological or physical depression. Discontent is damaging to the spiritual life of the believer.

It breeds frustration, anger, and envy. It disturbs love, destroys relationships, and disrupts spiritual growth. But it is *not* the same as depression.

Other Christian authors have also misunderstood the nature of depression, insisting that it should never be a part of the Christian's experience. Some even go so far as to say it is "sin"! These mistaken writers have failed to adequately discriminate between depression and other forms of unhappiness. The result is that this global condemnation of depression has caused much pain, increased suffering, unnecessary self-condemnation, and excessive guilt feelings for the many unfortunate victims of this malady—to which we are *all* vulnerable.

To illustrate, let me relate to you a story told to me by a woman I met while teaching a seminar for pastors and their spouses. This woman's husband, a minister in his middle thirties, had been deeply depressed. Believing that depression should not be a part of the committed Christian's life, and that his depression was a sign of God's rejection, he would spend long hours every day in prayer and the study of Scripture, desperately wanting to know why God had abandoned him. Naturally, this led to more depression. He refused to spend time with his family, and was barely able to perform his pastoral duties. Everyone was asking, "What's wrong with the pastor?"

Fortunately, one day the pastor became ill with influenza and had to visit the family doctor. His wife accompanied him and had the sense to tell the doctor of her husband's despondency. This led to the initiation of appropriate treatment and in six weeks the pastor was well on the way to full recovery and functioning normally again. His depression had a clearly physiological cause, and he responded rapidly and well to antidepressant medication.

Such misunderstandings and the consequent misery are extremely common in pastoral circles.

## Is Depression Sin?

Since this question is asked so often by sincere Christians, let me expand on my understanding of it.

I recently saw a letter which had been sent to the editor of a large denominational magazine from a dear and no doubt very sincere lady. She wrote, "I believe you should put the blame for all depression right where it belongs. The king of all depression . . . is the devil himself."

She then went on to admonish the readers who suffered from depression to recognize the work of the devil in their doubts and fears and to try "praising the Lord" and calling the devil the liar he is. This, she assured all, would guarantee anyone deliverance from his or her depression.

Her advice would probably be appropriate and effective in many other forms of unhappiness, but for the legitimately depressed individual it will not always be of help. While some aspects of depression may have sinful connotations, much depression is neutral in this arena. If anything, it is important to stress that one's spiritual life needs to be brought into the experience of depression, as it provides an invaluable source of therapeutic help.

The reason depression is so often connected with sin is that it is frequently confused with other forms of unhappiness. For example, depression is sometimes confused with "self-pity." While some self-pity may be present in depression, self-pity can exist entirely by itself and, of course, be very destructive to mental and spiritual well-being. Depression is also commonly confused with "doubting and lack of faith." While doubt is often a symptom of depression, it is secondary to the main problem. Unbelief may *predispose* us to depression, but it is not the same thing as depression.

## When Is Depression Sinful?

While I have stressed that we should not condemn all depression as being sinful, there are four aspects of depression that need to be considered when we think about the spiritual dimensions of this problem.

(1) *The cause of depression may be sinful.* While the depression itself should not be thought of as being sinful, the cause or trigger may many times fall within the domain of sin. Here, the depression is the consequence of some sinful act.

To illustrate, let us suppose that a married minister is counseling a woman. After a few months of seeing her regularly, he becomes very attracted to her. One day she decides to end the counseling relationship because she senses the minister's strong feelings of attraction and feels threatened by his subtle advances. She even stops coming to church. For a few weeks the minister searches the pews for her in vain, but she is not there! The minister then becomes depressed, the trigger being the woman's refusal to have anything more to do with him. Part of the depression is due to his guilt feelings over his behavior, but another and even more significant part is due to the loss of the object he admired and desired.

While this particular depression, as a response to the loss, is a normal reaction, the trigger involves sin on the minister's part, and spiritual steps must be taken in order for healing to take place. The minister must acknowledge that his desire for the woman is wrong

26

and, with God's help, overcome it before he can expect his depression to pass.

Does a depression which is the consequence of sin require any different treatment than that arising from other causes? Probably so. When depression is *caused* by sin it is important that the sinful cause be recognized and dealt with before the depression is allowed to pass; otherwise an important opportunity for spiritual growth is bypassed.

Separating the cause from the depression is extremely important in such cases. It is like separating pain from disease. The real problem is the disease, not the pain itself; the pain is simply the symptom of the disease. The problem with spiritual depression is its cause (the disease) and not the depression (the pain). It is the failure to differentiate between the depression itself and the underlying cause that creates most of the confusion in Christian circles about the nature and purpose of depression.

It is necessary that we as Christians recognize our responsibility to strive for righteousness. Since depression may sometimes be the consequence of our sinful behavior, we should be tolerant towards ourselves as far as the depression is concerned but "pull out all the stops" when dealing with its cause. Learning to do this is a part of our sanctification, and we have all the resources of the Holy Spirit at our disposal for this purpose. I think we will be surprised to find how often our depressions heal naturally and quickly when we have first dealt with the spiritual implications of their causes.

Sometimes, however, even when we follow the steps of recognition, confession, repentance, and acceptance by faith of Christ's forgiveness for the cause of the depression, we may still continue to feel depressed. This is because the biological changes that take place during a depression require time to heal. When the depressive process has been allowed to run its course, the feelings of depression can be expected to go away.

Unfortunately, the reverse is also true. Failure to deal with the sinful cause of a depression doesn't mean the depression *won't* pass. A person may come to terms with the loss and resolve the depression over a period of time without ever admitting or correcting the sinful act or thought. When this happens, however, the person misses a valuable opportunity to grow spiritually through the experience of depression.

(2) *Depression can be sinful when we fail to take necessary steps to treat it.* Many depressed individuals fail to take corrective psychological or medical steps to alleviate their condition, and consequently they perpetuate the depression. Not only is this masochistic; I consider it sinful! Many besides the depressed person will suffer because of this prolongation of misery. In a later chapter, we will explore just how

depression is perpetuated, but at this juncture let me stress that it is our responsibility, when we are depressed, to avoid unnecessary prolongation of the suffering. Not only can perpetuating depression significantly influence our spiritual well-being, but it creates potential for many other kinds of sin.

For those whose depressions are responsive to treatment by medication, choosing not to follow this treatment can cause unnecessary and unproductive suffering. If ministers, by not seeking treatment, allow their depression to be unnecessarily perpetuated, they not only do great harm to themselves, but also create obstacles to their ministry. They may even destroy their ministerial effectiveness altogether. Such neglect of "the temple of the Holy Spirit" must surely be sinful. It is the byproduct of the confusion about our emotions which is so prevalent in our culture. It is appropriate here to be reminded of James 4:17: "Therefore to him that knoweth to do good, and doeth it not, to him it is sin." I would suggest that the "good" for many depressed Christian workers is the knowledge that they can do something to get out of their depression.

(3) *Depression may be sinful when it is the consequence of giving power to others.* In my own life, I frequently find that a bout of depression can be triggered by the actions or words of another person. It's as if I have said to that person, "Here is my depression button. Press it whenever you like!" This tendency arises because we desperately want to be accepted, respected, loved, and cared for by others. Unfortunately this gives them tremendous power over us. I consider that it may be sinful to let other people have so much power over us that their approval or disapproval literally controls us.

Christian workers are probably more exposed to forces of acceptance or rejection than most other professionals. Parishioners, deacons, peers, spouses, and children are continually accepting or rejecting us. Sermons are evaluated, friendships continuously sought, behavior critically scrutinized, and judgments made about suitability, respect, friendship, spirituality, and competence (or so we believe). This creates many "depression buttons" that can easily cause havoc in our lives.

It is very easy to misperceive, misunderstand, and misinterpret the actions or words of others. We do not accurately perceive everything that happens in our interactions with others; we are bound to be selective in what we take in. Also, we will not always rationally and sensibly process what happens to us. The human mind, even when it is blessed with great intelligence, is by nature irrational, inconsistent, and subject to control and distortion by the emotions. Therefore much depression that comes from our interaction with other people will be based on our inaccurate perception or irrational assessment of what really happened.

But even if we do accurately perceive and process what others say and do, the fact remains that letting other people's words and actions depress us means that we have given them too much power over us. "They" can control our moods and determine our actions. We give other people this power when we need their approval excessively or when we want to impress them with our greatness, competence, and indispensability.

You will recall that John, in his Gospel, warned about the tendency to give others too much power over us. In commenting on why many of the chief rulers who had believed in Jesus would not confess him openly, he said, "For they loved the praise of men more than the praise of God" (John 12:43). I believe that this is a major cause of many depressions.

(4) *Depression can be sinful when we fail to rise up from our depression at the appropriate time*. There is, within certain limits, an appropriate period of time for a depression to last. The depression must run its course and, provided it is left to itself, it will naturally pass away. The duration of a particular depression will depend largely on the significance of the loss, the manner in which the depression was triggered, and the ways in which it has been perpetuated.

Say, for example, I purchase a new car and then have an accident on my way home. I am bound to experience depressive reaction to this unhappy occurrence. If the accident is minor and involves damage only to the front fender, my depression will probably only last a few hours, since the loss is not that great. If, however, I not only severely damage the car but also cause injury to the other driver, I am likely to be depressed for a much longer period of time. In other words, the duration (and depth) of a given reactive depression is proportional to the severity of the perceived loss.

A part of the appropriate time for recovering from a depression is taken up with adjustments to the biochemical changes triggered by the depression (tight stomach, loss of appetite, fatigue); the greater the loss, the greater will be the extent of these changes. A part of the time is taken up with cognitively processing the loss—thinking about what has happened, evaluating the loss and what it takes to replace it. Slowly the loss is put in perspective. As this is done, bodily functions return to normal and in due course the person comes out of the depression.

This is essentially what happens every time we become depressed because of a loss. One cannot simply decide that there is no longer a need to be depressed and then switch it off, except perhaps in the case of very minor depressions. However, we can fail to let go of a depression when it is time. By exaggerating our guiltiness and blaming ourselves we can keep ourselves in a depressed state much longer than is normal. Sometimes we even enjoy being self-pitying and miserable. Perhaps we may be afraid to resume normal functioning for fear that another catastrophe will overtake us, and prolonging the depression relieves us of many responsibilities. Whatever the reason, there comes a time when we must rise up out of our sackcloth and ashes and get on with life. Failure to do this is destructive to ourselves and those nearest to us, and this can be sinful.

## The Danger of Interpreting All Depression as Sin

While I have expressed the view that there are factors that can either cause or prolong depression, and that these factors may have sinful connotations, there is a great danger in focusing too much on the sinful aspects of depression. When one is counseling a depressed person, it is particularly treacherous to be too preoccupied with questions of sinfulness.

The depressed individual is already likely to be experiencing intense guilt feelings. He engages in self-condemnation, believes that his sins are unpardonable, and is preoccupied with how terrible everything appears to be. Laying an additional guilt trip on him by insisting that there is or may be a sin component in his depression will only increase the guilt feelings and bring on deeper depression. Since the sufferer already feels alienated from God, the added guilt will only make matters worse.

It takes much wisdom to know when to confront an issue of sin. The wise counselor may be more effective when he or she leaves the matter to God and prays that the Holy Spirit will do his work of convicting. I, personally, am not convinced that I always know when a depressed person is being willfully self-destructive. I proceed, therefore, with great caution in making such judgments. Sometimes I come to the point that I feel completely convinced a depressed person is engaging in the perpetuation of a depressed state or that there is some other sinful involvement. At that point, I have no qualms about confronting that person. But most times I find it better to remain in a very understanding and less confronting mode of counseling.

Failure to understand how sensitive a depressed person is to the suggestion of condemnation—either from God or others—can have disastrous consequences. I know a number of well-meaning pastors who use too much direct confrontation in their counseling. They can easily provoke suicide.

In one case, a depressed young schoolteacher I was counseling decided to stop therapy. She had been invited to live in the home of her pastor while he tried to help her out of her depression. His approach was to insist that her depression was due to demon possession and that she needed continuous prayer to free her from the demon. He would frequently lock her in a room with himself and, for hours on end, pray for the demon to leave her. One night she walked out of the house and, in a deep state of despair, placed her head on a nearby railroad track and ended her life.

It takes an experienced and skilled counselor to know how to handle the spiritual components of depression. Ignorance of basic physiology and psychopathology and the attribution of spiritual causes to common emotional disorders can be very damaging. Most pastors and Christian workers would do better to leave the Holy Spirit to do his work of convicting and healing.

## The Effect of Depression on Spiritual Life

Spiritual factors may cause or aggravate depression, but depression can also influence the spiritual life of the believer. The influence can be either destructive or beneficial, although we tend only to think about the destructive side of depression's influence.

One of the most unfortunate consequences of depression is that it may drive us away from spiritual things. The symptoms of depression—the lethargy, loss of interest, and the low mood—are not conducive to maintaining interest in the spiritual side of life. Pastors who are depressed may begin to doubt their effectiveness and label themselves as "hypocritical" and "abandoned by God." Devout Christians who become depressed often stop praying and studying Scripture, although depression can also drive a person to a preoccupation with Scripture and prayer. (If there is a retreat into religious activity it is often of the unhealthy variety that only raises the level of guilt and self-condemnation without offering the promise of redemption. Unfortunately, a depressed person seldom enhances his spiritual life through the experience.)

The abandonment of spiritual things must be seen as a symptom of the depression, which robs the individual of the concentration needed to focus on spiritual matters and distorts the awareness of God and. Scripture. God knows and understands this; so should anyone attempting to help the depressed person. Depression functions like a pair of dark glasses; it makes everything—including the spiritual life—look dark and bleak. It is important to remember that this bleakness is a product of the depressed perception and should not, therefore, be trusted! When the depression lifts, interest in spiritual matters will probably return.

# 4

## THE MANY FACES OF DEPRESSION

Depression can take many forms, ranging from the minor "Monday morning blues" and the fluctuating mood swings so common in many individuals to the most severe form of depression we know—the "manic depressive psychosis," now called "major affective disorder" in the latest *Diagnostic and Statistical Manual* of the American Psychiatric Association. (The term *affective* is roughly equivalent to the word *emotional*; depression is called an "affective disorder" because it is primarily a disturbance of the emotions. When a disturbance of the thought processes occurs, as in the case of schizophrenia, the disorder is no longer considered to be depressive per se.)

Everybody experiences the milder forms of depression to some degree; it is unrealistic for any human being to expect to be free of these. Depression can be any of the following:

(1) *A symptom*—the consequence of some illness or the side effect of medication. For example, it is very common to feel depressed when you have influenza. Depression is also a problem in many of the endocrine disorders, and is very common in women who take birth control pills. People who are being treated with antibiotics may also experience some depression as a side effect.

Depression in these instances is essentially protective; it may serve the function of withdrawing the affected person from his environment so as to conserve energy and assist the immunological systems of the body in resisting the illness. Such a depression requires no specific treatment. When the disease is over or the medication discontinued, the depression will usually end.

(2) *A disease*—the primary problem and not just a symptom of some other illness. The severe psychotic depressions fall into this category.

They are disorders in their own right. While the specific underlying cause has not been unequivocally pinpointed, research clearly indicates that some disorder of body chemistry is the primary cause of this kind of depression.

(3) *A reaction*—entirely psychological in origin. This kind of depression is triggered by awareness of something that is happening in the environment. This awareness may be unconscious, although in using this term I don't mean to imply the sinister function many psychoanalysts impute to it. By *unconscious* I merely mean that it is "below the level of conscious thought."

Most of what I will discuss in this book will be specifically directed toward this last category—depression which is a psychological reaction to environmental causes. These depressions are accordingly called "reactive depressions." Since the environmental cue has to be perceived and evaluated, the role of cognition (the way we think) in the triggering of depression is extremely important. For a further discussion on this important aspect of depression, I refer the reader to chapter 3 of my book, *Feeling Free*, (Englewood Cliffs, N.J.: H. Fleming Revell, 1979), which deals with the ways our thoughts cause emotional reactions.

## Other Types of Depression

We have looked at depression as a symptom, as a disease in itself, and as a reaction to something in the environment. It may be useful at this point to provide a summary of other types of depression before we proceed to discuss the most common form—the reactive—in more detail:

(1) *Neurotic depression.* Sometimes in a clinical situation we encounter an individual who is seriously incapacitated by depression or who habitually uses depression to escape or avoid responsibilities. We refer to this as a "neurotic depression." Here the depression has become habitual. Primarily it is a defense against anxiety, and the symptoms can become a way of forcing sympathy and support out of otherwise uncooperative and misunderstanding spouses, parents, or children. It is less a true depression and more a manipulative ploy. It is deeply entrenched, however, and requires skilled professional help for treatment.

(2) *Endogenous depression.* Endogenous literally means "from within." One of the more significant research finds of recent years is the discovery that prolonged stress can seriously disturb the biochemical functions of the body; stressful experiences can change our body chemistry. These changes can become long-term and produce

continuous states of depression even when the source of stress is removed.

Evidence of this kind of influence by social factors on biology represents a major breakthrough. A similar discovery has also been made in the area of pain. For instance, it has been demonstrated that merely believing a placebo has the power to remove pain actually increases the normal pain-killing chemistry of the brain. The old adage of "mind over matter" may have some credibility after all.

The implication of these discoveries is that the concept of "endogenous" depression, that is, depression which has its origin from within the body and not from the environment, may be legitimate. For many years, the existence of endogenous depression has been accepted only by some mental health professionals, who believed these depressions (without any apparent causal link to the external world) were caused by complex unconscious mental mechanisms such as repression, regression, and the like. But more and more we are recognizing that defects in body chemistry, specifically in the neurotransmitters that link nerve to nerve, may cause depressions which, while not always serious, are nevertheless incapacitating to some degree. Fortunately they respond well to treatment with antidepressant medication.

A very simple test has been devised in recent years to identify which types of endogenous depression will respond well to medication. This test will be discussed in chapter 10 when we deal with the treatment of depression.

Before it was understood that depression can be brought on by stress and biochemical changes, Christian workers who suffered from such depression often spent a lot of time and energy on unnecessary and fruitless searches for psychological or spiritual reasons. As a result, their depressed condition was only exacerbated by feelings of guilt and failure. Now treatment with antidepressant medication, plus adequate training in understanding the nature of their depression, setting limits on stress levels, and taking care of their bodies has revolutionized their lives. They feel normal again and can function more effectively in the glorious ministry to which they have been called.

(3) *Depression as helplessness.* Dr. Martin Seligman, a prominent psychological researcher, has explored the importance of "helplessness" in all human experience, but particularly the relationship of "learned helplessness" to depression. He has postulated the idea that when one feels helpless in a specific situation or in general, a negative mindset is created which in turn leads to depression. When "control" is reestablished, the depression abates.

Much of the helplessness that leads to this kind of depression is "learned." In other words, the individual has a series of experiences that cause him to believe that nothing he does makes any difference to the outcome of a life event. It is like driving an automobile with steering that is not connected to the wheels; the car goes where it wants to go and turning the steering wheel has no effect. This feeling of no control over the outcome of circumstances leads to a loss of hope and to depression. Even when an obvious solution to the situation emerges, the individual, having learned helplessness, does not try to do anything constructive.

This concept has been used to describe why wives who receive batterings from abusive husbands often do not take steps to leave them. But learned helplessness is not a phenomenon affecting only battered wives. I have counseled with many ministers who have become depressed because of learned helplessness. They feel they have lost control, that circumstances are against them, that there is nothing they can do to change anything. And so they resign themselves to a passive state in which they simply accept all the abuse that is handed to them.

The solution to these states of helplessness, of course, is to take corrective action and to resume control of one's direction in life. The depression and despair then rapidly vanish. But this is difficult for a person who has learned helplessness to accomplish alone. Often professional help is necessary to reverse the habit of helplessness.

## Mood-Swing Cycles and Depression

Occasional sadness, discouragement, pessimism, and a sense of hopelessness about being able to cope with or improve life circumstances are very common emotions. We are all prone to having such depressed feelings periodically, and it is important that we not misunderstand them. These periods of feeling "down" sometimes alternate with periods of elation and may resemble the cyclic pattern of the manic-depressive disorder. In fact, it is easy *to believe* that these mood swings are minor manifestations of a more serious disorder. But this is not so! These milder—and quite normal—fluctuations in mood are known as *cyclothymia* and are not in any way related to the manic-depressive psychoses.

For some, these natural cycles of mood swings reflect a natural biological rhythm. I do not mean a "biorhythm" in the popularized sense. Biorhythm charts which can be purchased almost everywhere are peddled to gullible people who don't realize how oversimplified the idea is. But complex biological changes *are* constantly going on in the body.

For women, there is a biological cycle of "ups" and "downs" which is well recognized and accepted. A high level of estrogen in the blood at certain points in the menstrual cycle will provide feelings of wellness and even elation, followed by deep "lows" and feelings of irritability when the level drops just before menstruation. A similar emotional "letdown," the "postpartum depression" which often follows the birth of a child, is caused by the dramatic biological and hormonal changes which take place once the baby has been removed from the mother's system.

The body is constantly coping with infection and dealing with conflict or stress. These defensive functions go on automatically and without our awareness, except for when we are presented with a bout of "low" feelings. After a while, the defensive function passes and we feel good again, even elated, only to find that the cycle repeats itself once more. These are all normal cyclical variations in mood accompanying physiological changes. They are not cause for alarm or for any special attention, except to let the body do its work.

Provided we don't misinterpret these cyclic fluctuations and don't cause ourselves more unpleasantness by overreacting to them, they are self-limiting, natural, and necessary to a healthy mind and body. We will be happier persons if we let God's natural laws take their course.

## Recognizing the Different Kinds of Depression

At other points in this chapter I have already mentioned some of the symptoms for different kinds of depression. For the sake of completeness and clarity, let me now bring these together and draw out the differences between them. I will confine my discussion to what I consider the four major categories of depression:

(1) *Psychotic depression.* Here, the degree of depression is very profound. Everything seems gloomy and hopeless, although the person may try to conceal the symptoms ("smiling depression"). The person reports a general loss of vitality, loss of interest in normal activities, and lack of energy. Unusual withdrawal from social activities is always present. Work, home activities, and personal health and appearance become greatly neglected.

What characterizes the psychotic depressions most is that the symptoms are so severe that the sufferer cannot go about his normal life. Feelings of guilt, remorse, self-reproach, and self-deprecation are so exaggerated as to seem delusional. The illness may be interpreted as a form of punishment for past sins, real or imagined. The person feels despised and suspects that everybody is accusing him of sinning. The individual is totally absorbed with himself and may report strange feelings or sensations.

This form of depression often comes on very rapidly (one to four weeks) and the incidence rises with increasing age. There is seldom any precipitating event—the disorder strikes like a bolt of lightning out of the sky.

There are two variations of psychotic depression. One is called bipolar because it shows a fluctuation over many months from depression to extreme elation ("mania") and back to either normality or to depression again. It is also called "manic-depressive psychosis" and it responds well to treatment with lithium carbonate. The other form is called unipolar because it only involves depression. Antidepressant medication is effective in its treatment.

At this point I want to sound a warning against self-diagnosis or lay diagnosis of psychotic depression. The description I have given here is for informational purposes only and is not sufficient for diagnosis or treatment. If you suspect a psychotic depression in yourself or in someone close to you, the best thing to do is to consult a competent professional right away. Treatment is painless and very effective in most cases, although it may require hospitalization. Sometimes symptoms of severe depression can be caused by physical disorders, and only a trained clinician can distinguish between possible causes.

It is also important to note that this kind of depression is relatively rare and not generally believed to be on a continuum with other varieties of depression. In other words, there is no reason to fear that mild forms of depression will lead to the severe psychotic forms.

(2) *Endogenous depression.* This kind of depression shows some of the symptoms described above, but with much less severity. Since many ministers and helping professionals may experience mild-to-moderate or even severe forms of endogenous depression, I will give a detailed account of its distinguishing features:

—The most important feature is that, even after detailed probing, the depression seldom proves to be related to any life event. Sometimes there is a minor connection, but the depression appears to be an exaggerated response to an unimportant event. It is especially important that a minister understand this. Because of the complexity of his relationships with people in his congregation, he could easily begin seeing in them the cause of his depression.

—It is frequently found that other members of the family (parents, near relatives) are also troubled by endogenous depressions.

—The depression is often accompanied by agitation, restlessness, and nervousness rather than by the "slowing down" that characterizes other types of depression.

—The symptoms appear to be worse in the morning and tend to get better as the day progresses, with evening being the best time.

—Sleep patterns usually involve easily falling asleep but wakening early and being unable to go back to sleep again. During this time the mind is overactive. Arising in the morning, the sufferer feels tired and jittery, with no sense of having rested. Chronic fatigue may be present.

—There may be intense, spontaneous, and agitated crying spells. One frequently hears the person say "I just want to cry all the time."

—Self-esteem may be completely lost. The person feels insecure, unsure, and empty. Decisions are difficult to make, memory is poor, and there is little ability to concentrate.

—Often there are complaints about stomach and bowel functions, chest pains, headaches, and loss of sexual interest.

—Suicidal thoughts may be present and death wishes intense.

—Interpersonal relationships are disturbed, social withdrawal and isolation is common, and the attitude is often "I don't care."

These are the typical signs of endogenous depression. Sometimes the problem is experienced as "low grade"; in these cases it is mildly in the background most of the time. More commonly, it is experienced as bouts lasting from two to twenty-six months if untreated. The onset may be fairly rapid. Fortunately, this form of depression responds well to treatment with antidepressant medication.

One form of endogenous depression is known as "involutional melancholia." Attacks of this form of depression usually occur for the first time in late middle life. It is most common in women around the time of the menopause, when it is also accompanied by anxiety, restlessness, agitation, and severe feelings of guilt.

(3) *Neurotic depression.* This form of depression is a lifestyle used to avoid anxiety, to escape responsibility, or to win sympathy and affection. In this kind of depression, the symptoms seem to be inappropriate or exaggerated responses by the person to his or her current life situation. Its onset is very gradual (over many years) and it may involve a wide variety of symptoms. Neurotic depression is very common in elderly people. In many respects the disorder is not a true depression and the person can be easily distracted from his symptoms.

(4) *Reactive depression.* This is the depression of everyday living. There is usually a clearly identifiable trigger or precipitating event, although the trigger may not always be readily discernable at first. The complexities of the particular loss which precipitates the depression can be very subtle and may not be fully grasped by the depressed person. Sometimes the "loss" is actually an accumulation of many minor losses or unsatisfactory life experiences. The physical and psychological symptoms of reactive depression are similar to those of

the other depressions, but delusions are clearly absent. There is good contact with reality, although some distortion in how the world is perceived may be present.

A person experiencing a reactive depression will usually show both physical and psychological symptoms. Some of the physical symptoms may include the following:

— The most prominent physical symptom is a slowing or "retardation" of activity. The person feels lethargic and does not want to engage in any physical activity.

— Disturbances of sleep and appetite follow. As an escape from the depression the person may want to sleep all the time or nibble away at food, or the depression can cause sleeplessness and loss of appetite (which is the more common response).

— Physical complaints may emerge. Commonly a knot in the stomach is reported, with disturbances of the bowel.

— There is usually a decrease in sexual interest and activity.

— In the more severe forms, personal appearance may be neglected.

Psychological symptoms of a reactive depression may include:

— The individual may be preoccupied with the loss that originally caused the depression (if this is known).

— There is a loss of interest or pleasure in usually satisfying pursuits. Hobbies, recreation, and work lose their power to arouse enthusiasm. Ambition is diminished.

— Feelings of inadequacy may arise, with or without loss of self-esteem. Self-esteem is not as severely affected as in the endogenous depressions.

— Social withdrawal isolates the person from friends and relatives. The individual does not want to see or talk to anyone, and prior social commitments are often cancelled or avoided.

— There is a strong feeling of guilt which takes the form of self-blame. This tends toward self-pity and a preoccupation with how terrible life is.

— Death thoughts occur only in the more severe reactive depressions when suicide can become a preoccupation. Even when suicide is not being seriously contemplated, these death thoughts may serve to reduce the anxiety accompanying the depression and provide fantasies of escape.

— There is diminished ability to think or concentrate, resulting in slowed thought processes and indecisiveness.

— The depressed feelings tend to be worse in the evenings and better in the mornings. (The reverse of endogenous depression.)

In many Christians there are also spiritual symptoms of reactive depression. These may run to two extremes. Either the person will

39

withdraw from God, blaming much of his problem on God's rejection of him and feeling an intensified guilt, or the individual may become obsessed and preoccupied with spiritual things, spending long hours in prayer and Bible study. Although this preoccupation may be regarded by observers as a healthy spiritual exercise, it may, in fact, be only a way of escaping from the symptoms of depression and may prolong the suffering unnecessarily by not allowing the natural healing process to take place. This is not to say that prayer and Scripture cannot be helpful to someone who suffers from a reactive depression, but care should be taken to ensure that these exercises are undertaken in a healthy and healing spirit.

One last point about reactive depression should be emphasized. It does *not* respond to treatment by antidepressant medication. Only when an endogenous element is involved (and reactive and endogenous depressions can easily overlap) is an antidepressant effective as treatment.

## How a Reactive Depression Occurs

Another way of understanding reactive depression is to examine how it occurs in people. The sequence is shown in Figure 1.

It is remarkable how even psychologically sophisticated people often overlook the following two facts: (1) We respond to what we *perceive* as happening in our environment, not to what is *actually* happening; and (2) after we have processed the perception in the light of our previous learning history, experience, biases, and so on, our minds pass the final outcome on to the rest of our bodies, and the feelings of depression we then experience are the *sum* of *all* the changes in the brain as well as in the rest of the body.

Many people erroneously believe that feelings are just "in our heads." We forget that an emotional disorder such as depression, even though it is triggered by psychological factors, finally becomes a physiological disturbance as well.

In a reactive depression, psychological factors may play two important roles:

(1) *They may precipitate the depression.* While they may seem to take only a fraction of a second, the perception of what is happening in the environment and the subsequent processing of the perception are nevertheless psychological processes which may bring on depression.

(2) *They may perpetuate the depression.* It is here, in the perpetuation of depression, that most neurotic forms of the disorder develop and that the greatest potential for sin exists. We can prolong what would otherwise be a minor depression of short duration by persisting in

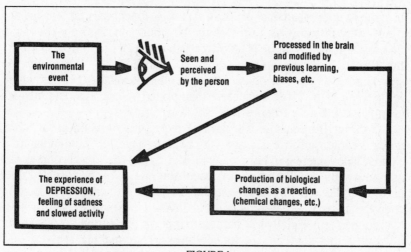

FIGURE 1
The sequence of events in the perception of loss.

erroneous and illogical ways of thinking and reasoning. The habit patterns for this tendency are learned early in life and are often deeply ingrained in the personality. Is it any wonder that the apostle Paul suggests that we could transform our whole nature by letting our minds be remade? (Rom. 12:2, NEB).

## Depression and the Grieving Process

We usually think of grief as the psychological process following the death of a loved one. While death is perhaps the greatest loss we can experience, it is in fact different from other losses only in severity and in the fact that our culture teaches us how to deal with loss through death by setting up very specific rituals which aid the grieving process. People who experience the loss of a loved one are given permission to feel their loss very deeply and are provided with an environment of support and sympathy. As a result, the average person adjusts to even the severest of losses through bereavement remarkably quickly. Occasionally in clinical practice we will encounter an individual in whom the grief process has gone wrong, but such instances are surprisingly infrequent.

While grief itself would not by conventional standards be depression in a clinical sense, it is still fundamentally a reactive depression. The grieving process is what depression is all about. In fact, it is possible to gain a clearer understanding of the nature of depression by viewing all reactive depression as a grieving process.

If we look at reactive depression this way, it becomes far less mysterious and confusing. In terms of the psychological and physiological processes involved, there is no difference between dropping and breaking a prized camera and the death of a loved one—except for the significance of the lost object and the intensity of the feelings which follow. We value loved ones more than prized belongings. But the loss of either can cause a depressive reaction.

Death may force us to experience a reactive depression in its purest and most intense form. The grieving person "turns off" on all external events, loses interest in hobbies or work, regrets the loss, becomes sad and angry, but finally comes to accept the reality of the loss and thus gives up grieving. This is essentially the same sequence we engage in over the loss of a pet, a job, or a favored position of status; over botching a sermon delivery; being separated from a friend or a spouse; imagining that someone no longer loves us; or making fools of ourselves at a committee meeting. Grieving is what reactive depression is all about! True, there may be a difference in intensity but the *process* is the same.

Our culture does not allow us to grieve over nondeath losses as easily as it allows us to grieve over death. If we fail an examination we are told that we should be "big enough to take the good with the bad." If we lose a relationship, we are told "There are other fish in the sea." If we miss an opportunity for improvement or a better preaching appointment we're told, "Don't overreact; other opportunities will come your way." In general the world is intolerant of our reactions to loss. Consequently our grieving is interfered with and our depression is thus prolonged. (I suspect that this is done primarily so that others can avoid their own discomfort at being in the presence of our grief.)

Subtly, but very definitely, our culture short-circuits the grieving process, and therein lies much of the trouble we have with depression. We fail to realize that grieving, whether over bereavement or other forms of loss, is part of an important adaptive process. God in his wisdom has created us to experience reactive depression as a way of coping with the many losses that life deals us. Resisting, fighting, resenting, or aborting this grieving process only leads to more depression and, as we will see later, the intensification of our misery.

## Depression as a Normal Response to Loss

At this point I am ready to stress the most important concept of all in learning how to deal with reactive depression. Simply stated it is this: All reactive depression is, in some way, a *response to loss*.

With this concept we can account for nearly all reactive experiences.

It is the simplest and easiest way to conceptualize the cause of depression. And I believe this concept is consistent with how depression is presented in Scripture.

The idea that reactive depression is a response to loss has been with us a long time. Freud espoused it, as do many other theoreticians. The loss can include a sense of deprivation or shame. It can be a loss of face and of feelings of worthiness, or it can be a state of helplessness involving a loss of control. There is hardly any form of reactive depression that cannot be seen in terms of loss. This, therefore, provides us with an important principle on which to base a method of coping with depression. In chapter 6 of this book we will look at this principle in more detail.

## Predisposition to Depression

It is generally accepted that certain people have an innate predisposition to depression—although how this comes about and operates is not clearly understood or agreed upon. I personally see this innate tendency toward depression as operating to *aggravate* the depressive response, not to *cause* it. In other words, I believe innate factors may make one person more apt to become depressed in a particular situation than another, and may even increase the depth of a particular depression, but it takes something in the psychological environment to trigger the process in the first place. Innate and psychological factors therefore work hand in hand.

For the purpose of illustration, let us suppose that we have two extreme types of people—Type X and Type Y. The Type-X person has certain innate features such as stable body chemistry, has learned how to cope with normal stress, disappointment and conflict, and is in all respects psychologically healthy. (Such an "ideal" person probably doesn't exist, but I suppose there must be some around who come close to this.) The Type-Y person, on the other hand, has a biochemical system that, for undetermined reasons (past experiences or physical factors, perhaps) responds easily and in an exaggerated manner to the triggers of depression. How will these two extremes of people experience depression?

Both will begin to experience depression when a certain loss or deprivation threshold has been exceeded. For the Type-X person, however, this threshold will be stable and within certain fairly predictable limits. Fluctuations will be minor and will be due to fatigue and other stress factors. The greater and more personal the loss, the greater will be the depressive reaction.

In contrast, the Type-Y person will have a low loss threshold. This threshold may fluctuate drastically from day to day, depending on factors such as fatigue, diet, and environment. Little losses may sometimes cause little depressions, but at other times big depressions—and there will be no consistent pattern. The depressions may seem paradoxical and may even appear to have no consistent relationship to the loss.

Most of us fall somewhere between the two extremes of the Type-X and Type-Y persons. Whether we have a stable disposition with a high threshold for loss or a low and variable threshold that responds easily and excessively to loss, the centrality of loss as the trigger of depression remains and needs to be understood. A clear understanding of our own unique threshold levels and whether we are closer to being Type-X or Type-Y persons will help each of us in our ability to cope with loss and depression.

# 5

## THE PURPOSEFUL NATURE
## OF DEPRESSION

Central to our discussion of depression has been the idea that "normal" depression has a purpose. It serves an important function for us both physiologically and psychologically. We miss God's intelligent creative purpose when we do not understand or accept this. Much misery for both pastor and people is caused by believing that depression is purposeless, unnecessary, and always destructive or undesirable.

This is not to say that we must welcome or deliberately create depression. On the contrary, I believe we should strive to eliminate as much depression from our lives as possible. Many depressions are responses to inappropriate or misperceived losses and, even when the loss is legitimate, it is possible to unnecessarily prolong our suffering through illogical and irrational thinking.

### Depression is Easy to Misunderstand

Many Christian workers have bouts with depression that are aggravated and intensified by feelings of guilt and failure stemming from erroneous notions about the nature of depression. There is a general lack of appreciation of the purposeful function of depression in Christian circles.

One minister told me how one situation always made him depressed. His wife had a busy schedule of church activities and worked as a teacher at a local school. This often necessitated her being away from home at the time he arrived home from work.

His daily ritual was to arrive home in the late afternoon, take a short break, have supper, and then complete whatever evening responsibilities he had scheduled. But if, when he entered the home, his wife was not waiting for him, he would become deeply depressed. He would then go to the bedroom and lie on his bed until she returned. Sometimes he would leave the house and drive his car aimlessly around the city for thirty or forty minutes until he thought his wife would be home. Naturally, when he did eventually return home he would be upset, angry, depressed, and noncommunicative.

This behavior caused a lot of marital conflict. He would never tell his wife why he became angry, and so the evenings of those days were spent in silence and sulking.

The minister became confused and increasingly frightened by his reaction as the years rolled by. He knew that there was a connection between his wife's absence and his subsequent depression, but he couldn't explain why his feelings were so intense. His guilt and sense of failure at not being able to control a simple reaction only served to increase his susceptability to depression. At the time he sought help he was in an almost continuous state of misery.

In therapy with him I emphasized that his depression had a purpose; it was a signal that something was wrong. He was experiencing a significant loss and he was not in touch with its ramifications. As we explored his early childhood, he was able to make the connection between his wife's not being home and his mother's frequent absence under similar conditions when he was a boy. He had, in fact, developed a conditioned response to the cue of her absence which had been transferred to his wife. We told his wife about his problem and established better communication about her letting him know when she would not be home. He then gave his wife "permission" not to be home when he returned (a technique called "paradoxical intention") and the problem abated in a matter of months.

My point simply is this: A person does not get depressed for no reason. The depression is a signal that something needs attention. It is like the squeal of a bearing that needs grease or the withering of a plant that needs water.

## Depression as Conservation of Energy

It is widely accepted that, in a seemingly hopeless situation or following prolonged frustration or stress, many forms of life eventually suspend activity and appear to "shut down" physically in order to conserve energy. For all practical purposes, they detach themselves from ongoing activity in their environment and withdraw into a lower level of functioning. After a time, when the threatening situation has passed or has been reassessed, the organism returns to normal arousal and functioning.

Humans are subject to the same defensive mechanism, but at a more sophisticated level. Much of what happens in depression can be understood in terms of "conservation of energy." There is strong research evidence to suggest that: (1) depression, especially in its milder forms, is adaptive; it forces us to make important adjustments to our changing and restricted world; (2) depression seems to facilitate the repair of our psyches following the experience of loss; and (3) depression, under many circumstances, is self-limiting.

In my opinion, these characteristics of depression are not accidental. They have been programmed into us by a Creator who carefully and meticulously organized our physiological and psychological constitutions so that, when they are functioning properly, they provide an effective system of coping with the complexities of human existence. They force us to come to terms with the limitations of our existence and to make the appropriate adjustments necessary for our survival.

The symptoms of depression—low mood, lack of energy, social withdrawal, and loss of interest in normal activities—force us to retreat from the demands of life so that psychic repair (presumably a cognitive task in which we make readjustments in our values, thinking, expectations, and hopes) can take place. When left to itself, the depression, provided that the biochemistry that supports it is not faulty, will limit itself and ultimately end.

Unfortunately, our physiological and psychological systems do not always function normally. Because human beings are contaminated by sin, breakdowns of body chemistry, faulty thinking, and the like, depression is not always self-limiting. The real problem is not the depression phenomenon in itself but our *tendency to prolong and intensify depression unnecessarily.* But the fact that we do not allow depression to do what it was designed to do does not invalidate its purposeful function. The fact that a bicycle has a flat tire doesn't mean that the bicycle has no function; it simply means that something is wrong with the bicycle. This analogy needs to be applied to our understanding of depression.

## The "Masking of Depression"

In order to allow depression to fulfill its purposeful nature, and in order to turn the pain and discomfort of depression into growth and maturity, we need to be able to recognize depression when it occurs. But this is not always as easy as it sounds. Frequently we fail to identify depression when it occurs in our lives; we will not admit we are depressed—even to ourselves.

There are many reasons for this. One reason is that many of us have a strong need to be always "on top" of things. (Ministers and helping professionals are especially likely to feel this way.) Both internal and external forces often demand that we be self-sufficient and self-mastering, and this can easily lead to an intolerance of any evidence of imperfection. Often we set up exceptionally high standards for ourselves, develop powerful self-controlling behaviors, and as a consequence develop a tendency toward denial; it becomes hard for us to acknowledge that there is anything wrong. Many of us suffer, furthermore, from a characteristic common to most people in our culture—we force ourselves to overlook emotional cues.

But denial is not the only reason depression often goes unrecognized. Another reason it is frequently missed or misdiagnosed is that it can masquerade in forms other than the low mood, sadness, dejection, despair, or melancholy commonly associated with the problem. This is why some people can honestly claim that they are never depressed—they never feel low, "blue" or dejected. But clinical depression does not require that we feel "the blues." Depression may be so disguised that the sufferer is unaware that a serious problem exists. We call such a disguised depression a "masked depression," and refer to the various behaviors that may serve to cover up the underlying depression as "masks."

A masked depression can be dangerous because it so often goes unrecognized and unheeded. This can persist until a full-blown depressive episode erupts and incapacitates the individual. Since early treatment improves the prognosis for recovery, such a delay can be devastating. In this chapter, therefore, I will be listing some of the "masks" a depression may wear.

But first a word of caution: It is not safe to assume that anyone who exhibits one of the behaviors I will list here is necessarily masking a depression or destined for a major depressive breakdown. The discussion here is intended only as a guide to seeking professional help, not as a definitive diagnostic tool.

At this point I also want to make an important distinction between the terms *mask* and *symptom*. While the two are similar in some respects, *mask* refers more to the manifestations of the disguise, whereas *symptom* refers to the primary underlying disorder. A specific behavior, such as lethargy, may be both a symptom and a mask. As a symptom, it is the direct consequence of the depression and a part of the depressive process. As a mask it is used to disguise and divert attention from the underlying depression.

The specific behaviors used to mask depression differ according to sex, age, cultural background, and learning history. An adolescent may mask depression differently than an adult, a sophisticated socialite differently than a janitor. Since this book is intended to be a guide for a wide variety of personalities, I want to look first at the specific ways depression tends to be masked at different age levels before proceeding to a general discussion of the more common masks of depression:

(1) *Masking in infancy and childhood.* The erroneous but persistent idea that infants and children don't experience depression is an indication that depression in early life frequently goes unrecognized. In both infants and children, depressive elements can be masked by a slowing of normal development—both physical and psychological. Infants who are deprived of normal cuddling or touching show signs of emotional, physical, and intellectual retardation. They become apathetic, reject all advances, and later in life find it difficult to establish effective relationships. All of these may be masks for an underlying deep depression.

Disobedience, excessive lying, truancy, temper tantrums, and school phobias may be masks for depression in later childhood. It takes a skilled professional to get to the real cause of the problem, as these symptoms can also be related to factors other than depression.

(2) *Masking in adolescence.* The masks used by children to cover depression are also found among adolescents. Underachievement, frequent changing of school courses, failure to take examinations, dropping out of school, expressed fears of assuming adult responsibilities—all are typical masks for this age. Depression is highly likely to be a factor in the increased use of drugs and alcohol among adolescents.

A habitual pattern of behavior used to mask depression can become well established in the adolescent years and follow the individual for the rest of his or her life. The frequent use of physical complaints to avoid anxiety-producing situations (hypochondriacal tendencies) and the excessive use of anger to control others (angry personality) are common examples of such behavior patterns.

(3) *Adult masks of depression.* In our culture, adult masking of depression commonly takes the form of physical complaints focusing on a variety of body organs. Individuals whose depressions are masked by physical complaints become chronic visitors to doctor's offices. Psychosomatic disorders can also be caused by deep-seated and unrecognized depression.

The excessive use of pain-killers, of prescribed drugs such as sleeping medications and minor tranquilizers (Librium, Valium), or of alcohol can be a mask for depression in adults. These drugs are used to provide an artificial "lift" and cover the low mood. Behavior such as compulsive gambling and extramarital sex has also been found to be a mask for depression. Here the "lift" is obtained by engaging in stimulating behaviors, and the more risky they are the more they serve to conceal and temporarily ameliorate the depression. People who habitually rely on the excitement of illicit sex to mask depression may reach the point that they cannot function sexually unless the sex is associated with fear or a stimulating environment.

Ministers of the gospel are not beyond such behavior—they are human like everyone else. I recently worked with the wife of a missionary who was having an affair. Deep down she did not really want to be involved with another man, but she just couldn't seem to help herself. I recognized in her a deep-seated depression and hypothesized that this was the reason behind the extramarital affair. I began treating her for the depression and, as it lifted, her compulsive need for another man's attention dropped away dramatically. (Obviously, one cannot categorically connect all extramarital affairs with a hidden depression, but I firmly suspect that there is a strong connection in many cases.)

## General Masks of Depression

The common ways of covering depression that are not age-related are:

(1) *Anger.* Frequent and unprovoked outbursts of anger can be a cover for depression. While I don't believe in the notion that *all* depression is anger "turned inward" (a Freudian idea), I am convinced there are connections between anger and much depression. In reactive depressions, a loss not only begins the depression cycle; it also creates frustration. Frustration in turn leads to anger, so depression is almost invariably accompanied by feelings of anger. In the emotional confusion that follows, the depression and anger intermingle and cannot always be separated.

(2) *Compulsive work.* This can frequently be a mask for depression, especially in individuals who are not usually compulsive. Humans normally welcome the security that patterned, organized behavior provides. When the behavior is productively plugged into the socioeconomic system, we call it "work." When it is involved with experiencing pleasure, we call it "play." If life is deficient in providing the satisfaction of our basic needs, it is easy for us to overinvest ourselves in the only source of satisfaction that our culture has structured for us—we become obsessive in our work. When this happens, we become compulsive and lopsided; work becomes all there is to our life. We neglect to engage in recreational activities because these only help to

bring the depression painfully into the open. It is usually easier to hide depression in our work than in our play.

(3) *Work inhibition.* Work inhibition is the inability to use one's inner resources, strengths, and talents in a creative way. It may result from a fear of failure, but is also frequently a mask of deep-seated depression. A significant decline in a person's work level is always a sign of trouble.

Sometimes the depression is also masked by other kinds of work-related difficulties. The person may experience physical complaints that interfere with the job or may claim to be bored with the work. Some people may become preoccupied with finding other employment (for example, seeking another church in which to minister) or with changing vocations. Such a change may indeed be constructive, but only if the underlying depression is acknowledged and dealt with before the change is made.

Conflicts, work difficulties, and problems with specific individuals may be ascribed by the depressed individual to fatigue and overwork. But this fatigue is itself a sign that the emergency system of the body has been overtaxed. It is a warning that stress is turning to distress, and that the primary underlying conflicts must be identified and resolved.

(4) *Loss of ambition.* Closely related to work inhibition as a mask for depression is the loss of ambition. There is a loss of aspiration and dreams, of a sense of purpose and calling. Depression can be either the cause or consequence of such a loss.

Few people operate consistently on a level of effectiveness congruent with their talents and potential. Yet most have a sense of their own capabilities and recognize diminished effectiveness as transitory. Over time, a graph of our work effectiveness will show rises and falls which fluctuate, just as our emotions do. This is normal. But when it occurs frequently or is marked, the loss of effectiveness and ambition may be a mask for depression.

(5) *Compulsive overeating.* It is a well-known fact that food intake has a quieting effect on anxiety. Individuals who are subjected to severe life changes such as divorce, business failure, job loss, or severe conflict in relationships often rapidly become overweight. Their over-eating is a sign of the gathering depression. Sometimes this is short-lived but it can easily become a chronic defense masking a chronic depression. Treatment of this type of obesity must focus on the underlying anxiety or depression. Failure to do this is one reason many weight reduction programs do not have long-term success.

(6) *Loss of sexual drive.* Sexuality is so fundamental to human existence that, barring physiological causes, any serious impairment of

normal sexual functioning must be interpreted as a sign of emotional difficulty—frequently depression. The consequent anxiety about loss of potency may give rise, even in ministers, to thoughts of sex outside of marriage to "test" whether everything is normal. Often impotence is attributed to boredom or feelings of anger toward the spouse, but it is also a mask for depression.

## Depression and Adult Phases of Life

One help in recognizing depression when it occurs in the adult years is realizing that there are certain transition points in adult life at which depression is likely to occur. These are times in which psychological adjustment must be made to a new "stage" of life. There are usually physiological changes going on at these times as well, and this complicates the picture. Sometimes these physiological changes may actually bring on an endogenous depression. But it is possible they may also lower a person's resistance to other kinds of depression as well.

A well-known example of such an age-related susceptibility to depression is the adolescent period. Changes occurring in the sexual glands (gonads) during the adolescent period create biochemical changes that can play havoc with the emotions. Emotional "storms" in which depression plays a dominant role cause withdrawal, sulking, and other behavior problems—as every parent knows. But it is less widely recognized that adults go through life-stages in which similar major biological changes take place, and that at these times a person may be especially vulnerable to depression—a relatively minor loss may bring on a major depression.

(1) *Depression in middle age.* In middle age there are at least two points where depression is likely, and the well-publicized "midlife crisis" may be involved at either point.

The first occurs anywhere between the late thirties and early fifties and is the consequence of a growing awareness that youth is passing and ambitions may not be realized. The defensive reasonings of the twenties and early thirties as to why one is not being successful begin to break down. This may precipitate a frantic search for self-improvement and a great need for reassurance. Sometimes reassurance is sought from members of the opposite sex through close friendships, or even through full-blown sexual affairs.

The second point in midlife at which depression is likely to occur is the "menopausal" period (anytime after fifty) when the gonads begin to decline and cease their procreative function. This syndrome is more common in women, although men are also known to become depressed at this time.

Like adolescence, late midlife involves massive changes in the endocrine system that can bring on an endogenous depression or perhaps increase a person's susceptibility to other kinds of depression. Hormone-related emotional "storms" may make life difficult for a time. And fears of old age, loss of sexual potency, or retirement can also contribute to the likelihood of depression.

Many of these fears, of course, are unfounded. Menopause does not necessarily mean a loss of sexual interest or activity, any more than retirement means a loss of usefulness and worth. In fact, often the end of the reproductive phase brings new sexual freedom to a marriage, since the fear of pregnancy no longer exists. The quieting of the emotions, once a more stable endocrine system is established, also brings greater harmony to the couple and a rediscovery of their deep love for each other.

(2). *Depression in old age.* During the final stage of life, old age, men and women may find themselves especially prone to depression. Old age lowers resistance to depression and causes deeper and more extreme reactions to loss, since the underlying biochemistry of those parts of our physiology that are involved in depression no longer has the resiliency it once had. Deteriorating health may also significantly increase the possibility of endogenous depression.

It might be thought that the proximity of death would be a major cause of depression in the elderly, but often this is not the case. In fact, old age seems to bring with it a greater acceptance of the inevitability of death. I recently talked to an elderly lady who was about to undergo major surgery for the removal of a tumor deep within her brain and who was deeply depressed. The surgeons had been frank in telling this woman that the chance of survival was not high. As we explored her depression it became clear that she was more concerned about the decline of her faculties and about becoming a helpless burden on others than about whether or not she lived. I talked with her openly about death, which she was ready to accept. We prayed, and as we parted we both realized that we might never speak to each other again. But I was convinced that her deep depression was not due to inability to adjust to the thought of death. Her depression was due to her failing body.

The depression that occurs in old age is one price we pay for having bodies that don't last forever. But depression even at this point of life is still purposeful. It can serve to slow us down, to conserve our energy at a time in life when our energy may be limited. It can prompt us to mobilize our adaptive resources for the years that are left—years that can be very full and satisfying despite a decline in physical faculties. Finally, it can prepare us for the next major transition in our life—

death—reminding us that our earthly bodies are meant to be used up and discarded in favor of the new, depression-free bodies our Lord has promised us.

# 6

## THE CONCEPT OF LOSS
## AND THE DEPRESSION CYCLE

I stated in an earlier chapter that all reactive depression can be understood as a response to some kind of loss. Some professionals may see this as an oversimplification. But I believe much confusion, and hence much unnecessary emotional suffering, has been caused by a tendency in contemporary psychology to make essentially simple concepts sound complicated.

The truth of the matter is that, excluding the obvious physiologically based varieties, depression *is* generally induced by a specific set of life events, the most notable being a loss of some kind or an experience of deprivation. Therefore it is quite accurate to say the role of loss is central to an adequate understanding of common reactive depression. This idea is not new, of course, and as we will see later was clearly understood even by the apostle Paul in New Testament times.

In exploring the theme of loss as a cause of depression, however, we need to keep the concept broad. The general category of loss can include such widely different events as bereavement after death, separation from a person or pet, the theft of belongings, or deprivation of such personal qualities as self-esteem or self-control. The losses we experience can often be intangible and hard to pinpoint, so it is helpful to have a schema for analyzing them and ensuring that we do not overlook the less obvious types. (A model for understanding the various kinds of loss is given in Figure 2.)

### Concrete and Abstract Losses

At the most basic level, losses can be divided into the two categories of "concrete" and "abstract." Those losses that are tangible, that can

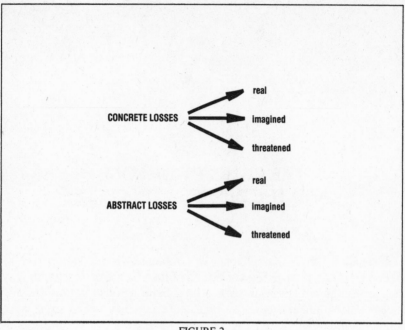

FIGURE 2
A model for understanding loss.

be seen and touched, are what we call concrete losses. This category includes losses of people, cars, jobs, pets, vacations, sermon notes, a favorite Bible, and the like.

Those losses that cannot directly be seen or touched are categorized as abstract. They include the loss of intangible realities such as love, control, self-respect, ambition, being in God's favor, freedom from undesirable traits, and so on. Such abstract qualities depend on our beliefs and value systems and can, of course, greatly differ in importance from person to person.

Abstract losses can be just as powerful in causing depression as concrete losses. In fact, by nature abstract losses tend to be more devastating than concrete ones. An abstract loss is harder to define than a concrete loss. Therefore it is harder to deal with rationally and often harder to accept.

For example, if the rear axle of my prized car breaks, as it did three weeks ago, I can deal with the loss (use of the car and the cost of repair) far more effectively than I can the loss of my eldest daughter's respect when I have been unfair to her. The first loss, a concrete loss, can be handled. The car can be repaired, or I can simply adjust to not having use of it. But the second loss is more elusive—an abstract loss.

How can I be sure I've lost my daughter's respect? Have I really been unfair, or is she being unjust in withdrawing her respect for me? Because my loss exists primarily in my mind, the product of many subtle factors, there is no way I can simply "fix" the problem or adjust to it.

## Real, Imagined, and Threatened Losses

Each of the two basic categories of losses can be further classified as real, imagined, or threatened.

(1) *Real losses.* Both concrete and abstract losses are "real" when there is no doubt about the fact that something has been lost. When my prized portable stereo cassette recorder is stolen, I experience a concrete, real loss. When I lose power through being overruled by a board or committee, or lose lack of acceptance from a person with whom I am having a personality conflict, I experience an abstract, real loss. When my manuscript for a book is rejected by a publisher, the loss I experience is both concrete (loss of royalties) and abstract (loss of ego satisfaction)—but it is nevertheless real!

(2) *Imagined losses.* Often, losses can be the product of our energetic minds, in which case they are categorized as "imagined." For example, we can imagine that we are responsible for almost everything that goes wrong in the church and take the blame, even if the problems aren't really our fault. We can imagine that people don't like us or that we are going to be rejected. We imagine catastrophe—and often become as upset as if the disaster had really happened.

Allow me to relate a personal incident. When my wife and I first moved to the United States we looked around for a home to buy. One day, while driving along the coast near Los Angeles, I saw a "For Sale" sign on the most gorgeous piece of land you can imagine. It had a beautiful sea view, it was level, and it had the potential for subdivision. I asked the realtor to find out how much the owner, now living in New York, was asking for it. Even though the price was extremely reasonable, I decided to submit a lower offer. I felt confident that, even if my offer was rejected, I could still buy the land at the stipulated price.

My imagination went to work. I drew subdivision plans in my head. I prepared a profit-and-loss statement (showing a lot of profit, of course) and I planned the home I wanted to build on one of the lots. While I waited for a response, I was on cloud nine. And then the reply came: The owner had decided not to sell the land at all. I was shattered! My depression lasted for a week. I had set myself up for a significant, though imagined, concrete loss; I lost what I didn't have. It is this tendency of our overeager, imaginative, and uncontrolled minds to betray us that gives rise to popular warnings like "Don't count your chickens before they hatch!"

Imagined abstract losses are even more common. We are snubbed, rejected, ridiculed, made fun of; our sermons are not appreciated, our management ability not respected, our financial acumen ignored—all in our imaginations, of course. We are careful to select from what we see and hear only those bits of information that support what we already suspect. Some people keep themselves constantly on the verge of depression over abstract, imagined losses.

Of course, it is ridiculous to allow our imaginations to make us so unhappy. So the way to deal with a suspected imagined loss is to "test its reality"—wherever possible, to convert an imagined loss to a real loss—because a real loss can be handled more effectively. For instance, a person who thinks he is being rejected should find out if it's true! An employee who suspects rumors are being spread about him should find out if it's true. A parent who suspects a child of being dishonest should find out if it's true. A few well-placed questions will usually produce the necessary information. Then the evidence can be carefully weighed and suspicions that are the product of the imagination can be rejected.

If an imagined loss can't be converted to a real loss, it should be discarded. The chances that the imagination is right are probably negligible! Correcting an overactive and suspicious imagination may be well worth the trouble of a period of counseling or psychotherapy. Intelligent prayer directed specifically at this problem may be even more effective, depending on how well the person knows himself and whether he knows how to cooperate with the Holy Spirit in therapeutic sanctification.

(3) *Threatened losses.* The third kind of concrete and abstract loss is "threatened" loss. Here the impending loss is real, but it is still too early to know when and how it will happen or even whether the loss will actually occur.

We experience such threats of loss when we have an elderly parent lingering at death's door, or when we discover a lump and must await the outcome of a biopsy or other test to see whether it is cancerous. No actual loss may have occurred, but there is a threat of a real loss hanging over us. Such losses can produce depression just as real or imagined losses can, and these depressions may be more unpleasant to experience simply because the depression can't *go* anywhere; we cannot accept or deal with a loss that hasn't happened yet! As a result, we are likely to be caught up in a self-perpetuating cycle which is triggered many times over. Threatened losses can also play on our imaginations more than real losses.

Life is full of potential for threatened loss. Ministers, because of their leadership visibility, easily become the target of much criticism. They are often blamed for everything that goes wrong in the church. After a few experiences of being blamed, they can become very sensitive to every minor failure, imagining that they will be held responsible for even the church mouse's activities. Threats, threats, threats—hanging over one's head like a guillotine about to drop! They represent loss of some sort, most of the time, and the effect of these threatened losses can drag on indefinitely if left unattended. Often a state of helplessness sets in and the recipient passively resigns himself to receive all the blame, punishment, and accusations that can be dished out without taking any steps to either defend or extricate himself from the destructive situation.

As in the case of imagined losses, the way to deal with a threatened loss is to convert as much threatened loss to real loss as possible. Careful attention must be given to avoiding the traps of imagination, catastrophizing, and exaggeration. Forcing threatened losses into real losses is sometimes possible by the appropriate use of confrontation so as to get clarity and information about a specific event. For example, we are far better off knowing whether or not we have cancer than having the threat of it hanging over our heads. Similarly, the many threatened losses of ministry are better dealt with if they are tested for reality.

Of course, there are some threatened losses we simply have to live with for a while. If a threatened loss is not imagined and cannot be converted into a real loss (for example, the serious illness of a loved one), the only thing to do is pray for the courage and endurance to get through the difficult time of waiting for the threat to be resolved.

It is natural to experience depression during such times; human beings simply were not designed to cope indefinitely with loss. So when we are faced with a prolonged threatened loss it is important that we be kind and gentle with ourselves, tolerant of our reactions—we need to "give ourselves permission" to feel as we do. It is probably a good idea to avoid heavy work schedules during such times, although the distraction of a hobby or travel could be beneficial. It can also be helpful to keep our minds on the larger perspective—reviewing life goals, clarifying values, trying to see the situation in terms of God's overall plan and purpose for our lives. And, of course, it is important to continue doing whatever can be done to keep the threat from going on any longer than it has to.

## The "Ideal" Depression Cycle

Although the concept of loss is the key to understanding reactive depression, it is also important to have some idea of the *process* of depression, sometimes called the "depressive cycle." Figure 3 presents the sequence of an "ideal" depression—one without any complicating factors. (Such a depression, of course, probably doesn't exist, but it is useful for the purposes of discussion.)

In the "ideal" depression cycle, the *trigger* is the moment the precipitating event reaches a level of awareness sufficient to be perceived as a loss. This awareness may occur immediately after the loss, or it may be delayed until full realization of the loss has taken place. Each of us will process loss differently, according to the meaning and value we place on the lost object or person. These differences are as unique as thumbprints and in some respects are fairly stable over time. (This predictability can help us avoid future depressions.)

Immediately following the awareness of the loss, we begin the state of being depressed. Complex changes occur in our body chemistry, certain parts of our brain are stimulated, and what results is the feelings and symptoms of depression. The depression eventually "bottoms out" at a depth appropriate to the degree of loss, and then recovery gradually takes place.

The time that it takes for the whole cycle will depend on the severity of the loss. Faster recovery follows smaller losses. Recovery is also

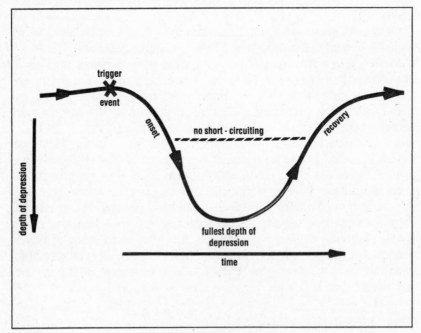

FIGURE 3
The "ideal" depression cycle.

determined by the cognitive processing of the loss (the way we "think it through").

## The "Typical" Depression Cycle

Few depressions, however, follow this "ideal" sequence. More typically, our experience is that shown in Figure 4.

In the typical experience of depression, the awareness of the loss is the trigger, as before, but as we become depressed, we create further reactions. We may think about the event that triggered the depression and thus create a series of secondary reactions.

For example, let us suppose a minister has just finished preaching. He believes he has flopped, so as he leaves the pulpit he feels a little depressed. He greets the members outside the church. A few positive remarks are made by respectable members of the congregation, so the preacher begins to feel better (the depression "bottoms out" the first time). He tells himself that maybe the sermon wasn't so bad after all. But just as he is starting to feel better, someone says, "The sermon

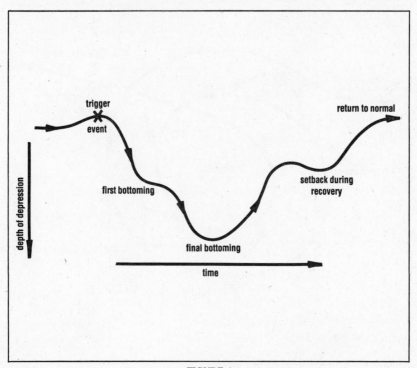

FIGURE 4
The "typical" depression cycle.

wasn't as good as last week's, but I don't suppose we can always get your best!'' The remark was meant to be reassuring but coming at that moment it causes the minister to feel a loss again, so the depression deepens.

The minister finally finishes shaking all those hands, breaks loose from other Sunday chores, and heads for home and lunch. Dare he ask what his wife thought about the sermon? What if she agrees with his perception of how bad it was? "Nothing ventured, nothing gained," he says to himself, "so let me test the water and see where I stand."

"Darling, tell me honestly. How did the sermon come across today?" If the answer confirms his fear, there could be a further deepening of the depression. If it reassures him and his loss was only imagined, he begins recovery, having "bottomed out" the final time. But further setbacks to the recovery may occur at any later point.

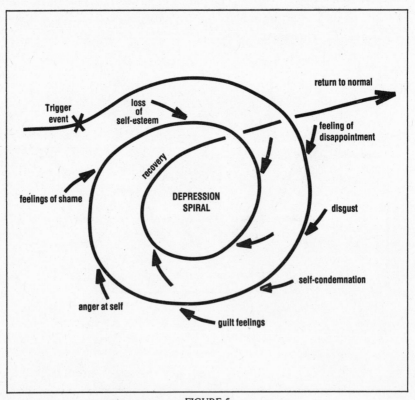

FIGURE 5
The self-perpetuating depression spiral.

## The Depression Spiral

A further complication of the normal depression cycle is the "depression spiral." What happens here is that a pattern of ever-deepening depression is set up. This is depicted in Figure 5.

In this model, as the depression develops, the individual begins to react to the feelings of depression by engaging in what is called "emotional chaining." The original emotion (in this case the beginning of depression) evokes all sorts of ideas in the mind of the depressed person: "What is happening to me?" "Why am I feeling this way again?" "Oh no, don't tell me I'm getting depressed again."

These thoughts, in turn, evoke more emotional reactions, so that the person leap-frogs or "chains" from one emotion to the next.

As Figure 5 indicates, the first reaction may be a feeling of self-disgust or self-blame. There are feelings of disappointment and self-hate. These represent further losses and add an extra impulse to the depression, causing it to deepen further. We may begin to feel guilty about being depressed. This is followed by anger toward ourselves, then shame, and this creates a further sense of loss and more depression. So a spiral pattern is established. We are now *perpetuating* the depression and it is no longer a "normal" experience. Fortunately, for most of us this spiral gradually loses its energy, slows down out of sheer exhaustion, and the process of recovery and return to normality slowly takes place. But sometimes the depression cycle can accelerate so rapidly that it "spins" out of control.

Some years ago I learned how to fly an airplane. One of the exercises we had to master was throwing the plane into a spin and then recovering from it. To spin the plane, one has to slow it down to stalling speed, kick the rudder to one side, and put the plane into a roll. As the plane spins it seems to point almost straight down and to twirl faster and faster—a frightening sensation the first time it is experienced. The spinning of a depression which is out of control is much like this. It gains momentum from itself, and once it starts it can take a person crashing all the way down to a major emotional breakdown. There is even a possibility of suicide if the spin isn't broken.

It *is* possible to recover from a depression "spin," however. This usually requires the seemingly paradoxical step of giving ourselves "permission" to be depressed. This cognitive step of "allowing depression" serves the important function of stopping the process of emotional chaining, and is very helpful in speeding recovery from even minor depressions. If it is permissible to be depressed, then why be disgusted with ourselves for responding the way we do? Giving ourselves permission to be depressed helps us gain control of the secondary reactions that can perpetuate a depression—reactions such as self-blame, disgust, guilt, and anger. And when these perpetuating factors are removed, the depression will eventually lift in the normal manner.

## A Depression Can't Be Short-Circuited

There is an appropriate amount of grieving to be done for every loss—and therefore an appropriate depth for every reactive depression. And, while we don't want to perpetuate any depression unnecessarily, it is important that every depression be fully experienced to its appropriate depth without any attempts to abort or "short circuit" the process (refer again to the diagram of the "ideal" depression in Figure 3).

One of the most callous things we can say to anyone who is experiencing depression is "Come on, snap out of it!" or words to that effect. Mostly, we say things like that not so much because we want to help the depressed person, but because we are feeling uncomfortable in their presence. It is *our* need that prompts us to advise others to pull themselves together. Our sympathetic responses are too sensitive to the pain of others and we want *them* to make *us* feel more comfortable.

Unfortunately, such advice not only is ineffective; it may actually *prolong* the depression by causing emotional chaining on the part of the sufferer. He or she may think, "See, I've done it again. Everyone is unhappy with me." Such an evaluation in turn triggers additional feelings of loss and still deeper depression.

There is no way a depression can be effectively short-circuited in the early stages. As we will see later, there may be effective ways to speed up the final, recovery stage. But pushing a person to recover from a depression too early is useless and may be harmful. A much better approach on the part of well-meaning parents, spouse, pastor, or friends of the depressed individual is an attitude of loving concern that says, "It's all right to feel the way you do. I understand, and will do everything I can to support you through this difficult time."

# 7

## THE PHASES OF DEPRESSION—
## ONSET

The typical depression consists of several stages or phases. These are usually clearly identifiable, although recognizing them may become tricky when there is more than one type of depression occurring at the same time or when a depression is retriggered by the memory of the original precipitating event. Learning to identify these phases can be a helpful tool for understanding how depression works and how to cope with it.

Figure 6 shows the phases of a depression. In the chart, point A represents the "trigger" of the depression. This may be the moment the person becomes aware of the loss or deprivation or it may be the beginning of an endogenous depression. Between points A and B there is the "onset" phase. Here, the complex biochemical and neurological processes that underlie the experience of depression are established. The rate of onset is a function of a particular person's physiology and the significance of the loss. For example, the greater the loss the more rapid the onset will be.

Point B represents the first low point reached. It is the beginning of the "middle" or "valley" phase and may come early or later in the depression. This point may then be followed by a temporary recovery period (from B to C) and by further depression (D).

Eventually this fluctuating middle phase begins to give way to the "recovery phase" (from E to G). Notice that in the period from E to F there may be what is called a "plateau"—a time when the depressed person is neither improving nor getting worse. Finally, recovery from the depression occurs at point G and the individual returns to normal functioning.

There are many variations to this pattern but generally we can speak

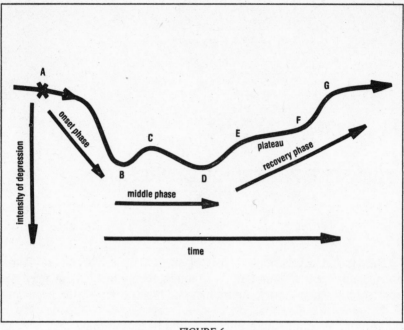

FIGURE 6
The phases of reactive depression.
(see text for explanation of points labelled)

of depression as consisting of the three major phases: onset, middle, and recovery. Each has important characteristics and hazards. In this and the next two chapters I will be exploring ways of coping with a "normal" depression at each stage. Then, in chapter 10, I will be looking at the option of seeking professional help for a severe depression.

Throughout this discussion, it is important to bear in mind that I am giving only a generalized picture of the depression cycle and that each individual will experience depression differently. It is fascinating, however, to note that a given person will tend to repeat the same pattern every time he or she becomes depressed. Like a fingerprint, the pattern of depression is characteristic of the individual. This knowledge can be helpful in treating the depression because it can predict what is to happen and show when intervention may be appropriate and helpful.

## Recognizing the Trigger of a Depression

Like all emotions, depression has a beginning point. Sometimes it is sudden; a depressed person may be able to recall the exact moment when the depression started. Sometimes it starts slowly and creeps up on the person like a mist, almost without his being aware of it.

However it begins, the first and perhaps the most important step in coping with depression is learning how to recognize this point of beginning. Knowing when a depression started provides the information needed to identify the cause of the depression.

In the case of a reactive depression (the most common kind), identifying the trigger event is a matter of recognizing the loss that has been felt—whether that loss is concrete or abstract, real, imagined, or threatened. It is important to remember, however, that what causes depression is not the loss in itself, but our *perception* of the loss. It is what the loss means to us in terms of our values, beliefs, attitudes, and expectations that determines how we will react to it and how deep the depression which follows will be.

Much of the way we perceive loss is determined by our past learning and experiences. We *learn* to attach meaning to objects and abstract ideas. Therefore, if we can modify the effects of our past learning on these meanings, we can improve our attitude toward many losses and thus either prevent them from becoming triggers for depression or shorten the depressions that do occur. (I know this because I've done it for myself. And I believe it is at this point, more than any other, that being a Christian believer can help protect us from unnecessary depression. Christianity can put our losses in an entirely new perspective by revolutionizing the meaning of past experiences and by providing us with an entirely new value system.)

One of the things that characterizes the depression-prone individual is the way he construes deprivation or loss. Typically he does two things wrong: (1) He misperceives many life events; and (2) he overgeneralizes or attaches extravagant meanings to loss.

Let me illustrate from a recent case how these points can operate in the life of a pastor. Joe is an experienced minister and leader in his denomination. Despite this prominence and a successful career that has spanned twenty years, he repeatedly experiences much discomfort through depression. He consulted me, and we spent some time exploring these depression bouts. What emerged was a picture I have often encountered.

Joe had a strong tendency to misinterpret what people say or do. This tendency bordered on paranoia at times because it had little basis in reality. He would spend long hours at night thinking about what Dr. Jones said during a committee meeting, evaluating why Mrs. Smith made suggestions for improving the order of the worship service, or whether the proposals of the youth pastor implied criticism of him.

Because Joe always needed to know what people were thinking

("where they were at" he called it), he would persistently—and some-times aggravatingly—seek information from others, but he seldom used this feedback constructively. He would be utterly devastated if it did not provide complete and positive support for his ministry.

Joe was, in effect, creating situations of loss over and over again in his mind. The most ridiculous aspect of it all was that *none* of the losses existed outside his head. They were all imagined!

I worked intensively with Joe to change these thinking patterns, and we were able to bring about some reduction in the frequency of his depressions. The steps I suggested he take are not difficult to learn and can be extremely helpful to anyone who finds himself frequently depressed:

(1) *Improve your awareness of being depressed*. As I have pointed out before, many people are so used to denying their emotions that they cannot even tell when they are depressed. A person who has this difficulty may need to recruit a spouse or a close friend to point out whenever he starts *acting* depressed. People who have a history of depression may need to list specific situations that trigger their depres-sion and then devise special systems to remind them where they tend to get hooked. Some people stick small round dots of colored paper on their watch dial or shaving mirror. Others place a small card in their wallet or handbag or a marker on their desk—anything that will cue them to ask themselves, "Am I depressed right now?" The habit of asking themselves such questions will help most people learn to iden-tify when they are depressed.

(2) *Identify the precipitating event and label it as the trigger*. This is not always easy. Some triggers become obvious as soon as the person acknowledges he is depressed. Others are more elusive. One helpful exercise is to take a moment to mentally trace the events of the previous hour (or longer, if necessary). "What did I do? Where did I go? With whom did I speak? What did I see? What did I read? What was I thinking about?" These questions, written on a card as a checklist if necessary, can serve to prompt the depressed person to consciously recall the event, thought, or awareness that triggered the depression. It's a good idea to pay special attention to minor depressions because they are likely to occur more often and will be easier to overlook.

A personal example illustrates how to do this. A moment ago as I was writing, my mind, as it so often does, wandered on to other things. After a while I suddenly came back to the present and realized I was experiencing a familiar feeling of discomfort in the pit of my stomach. My abdominal muscles had become tense and I had become fidgety. I stopped what I was doing and reviewed my thoughts of the past five or ten minutes. And then it came to me: My eldest daughter, who lives in an apartment not too far from our home, was experiencing problems with her car. She had traveled to another city the night before to attend a missionary rally and, since I had not heard from her, I was concerned. As soon as I identified the trigger for my depression, I felt a sense of relief. I knew what I had to do. I made a telephone call, confirmed that she had arrived home safely, and saved myself hours of discomfort. I was able to get my mind back on writing.

(3) *Use "reality testing" to determine whether you have misperceived the situation.* Simply stated, this means "check it out!" A depressed person shouldn't trust his own perception or imagination, but should ask a friend or spouse to evaluate the situation with him. Paranoid tendencies can exist in otherwise normal people, so it's important for each of us to be honest enough to confront these in ourselves. Sometimes the tendency to harbor unfounded suspicions and to misread situations defies self-analysis or the help of friends. If this is true, I strongly recommend professional help. This trait can be deeply ingrained in the personality and its origin can go back to the early stages of life. But a competent Christian psychotherapist can help! Life is too short and too precious to be darkened by paranoid suspicions and unfounded fears.

For Christians, these suggestions for learning to recognize and analyze the beginnings of depression need to be followed in an attitude of prayer and dependence on God's Spirit to lead us into the truth about ourselves. When we first try to follow them, we may not succeed, but they become easier with practice. The main objectives at this point are:

—To test whether there has been a loss significant enough to be depressed about.

—To diminish, or even remove, the power of the trigger to maintain the depression; and

—To speed up the onset phase of the depression if the loss is, in fact, real and significant.

## Dealing with Depression During the Onset Phase

During this period the complex interconnections between the mind and the body are set in motion and the various biochemical and neurological changes constituting depression take place. The rate at which the depression develops can vary from person to person and from situation to situation. If the loss is legitimate—a genuine and meaningful loss such as bereavement or losing a job—it is probably desirable that the onset take place as soon as possible after the loss so that the natural grieving process can run its course and healing can begin.

It is at this point, however, that the depression can begin to be unnecessarily perpetuated. During the onset phase particularly (although it can occur at any point during a depression), there is a tendency for further emotional reactions to be created; one emotion will give rise to another like an echo reverberating across a mountain valley. As I mentioned earlier, this is called "emotional chaining." It is illustrated in Figure 7.

Emotional chaining relies heavily on "self-talk" (the stream of thoughts about ourselves that continuously goes through our minds). It typically takes place as follows: As the individual perceives a loss and begins to feel depressed, he evaluates what is happening. Then he may ask himself, "Why am I feeling this way? What will others think of me?" The additional thoughts have a strong tendency to produce further emotional reactions. Feelings of anger, guilt, and self-condemnation can follow and be the springboards for still more negative emotions. Fortunately, in most cases the process of emotional chaining weakens and dies out. But, as we saw in the last chapter, it is possible for chaining to gain strength until it leads to a full-scale emotional breakdown—what is often called a "nervous breakdown."

A good example of emotional chaining is the case of a minister's wife I once knew whose husband betrayed her trust and his marriage vows and left her for another woman. This man was highly respected in his denomination and had even served as its president, but he gave up

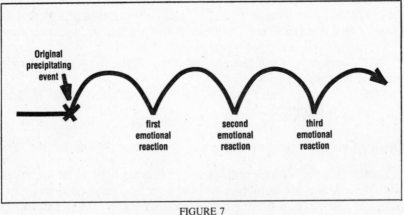

FIGURE 7
Emotional chaining.

his church, his reputation, and his marriage for the woman who has been his secretary for a number of years. (I know it sounds trite, but this is what really happened!)

How did his wife take it? She was devastated; the loss was more than she could bear. Her self-talk went like this: "He has humiliated me. How can I look my friends and family in the face? My life will never be the same again."

After a while her first emotions gave way to feelings of disrespect for herself. Her self-talk became: "I am nothing without him. He is the only man I've ever cared for. I can't live without him." With further chaining it became: "If I had been a better person, given him more love, and had been more understanding, this would never have happened." Finally the self-talk and feelings settled on self-condemnation and guilt.

As this woman moved from one set of negative feelings to the next, her depression became increasingly worse. With each chain she created more loss for herself until her emotional state was so bad she had to be hospitalized with runaway depression.

While her husband's abandonment certainly was a severe loss, this woman's emotional chaining considerably aggravated her depressive reaction. The secondary emotions, fed by catastrophic ideas such as "this is too much for one person to bear," and "this is a terrible disaster for me to experience at this stage of my life," only served to exaggerate her suffering. Emotional chaining undermined her ability to absorb the shock, experience normal grieving, and get on with her life.

To reduce the impact and reverberations of all losses, minor and major, it is a good idea for us to learn how to prevent emotional chaining in even the smallest of disruptive situations. Chaining is a habit. We are not born with it; we learn how to do it! And if we do it in some situations we are likely to do it in many. It is often founded on irrational patterns of thinking, and these must be confronted and modified before chaining can be stopped. The best time to work on this habit is during periods of relative emotional stability. When the problem is severe, it is sometimes more effectively dealt with in professional therapy, although I have known many ministers who have shown amazing ability to modify this tendency merely by understanding the phenomenon and keeping a watchful eye on their thinking and reactions.

## Thought Stopping

Since emotional chaining is carried out in the stream of our thought and through self-talk, any technique that can stop or redirect our thinking can be effective in preventing chaining. A most effective technique, known as "thought stopping," is used for this purpose. The basic goal of thought stopping is not to stop *all* thought but merely to direct the thoughts away from the troublesome area. You don't stop thinking, you only stop thinking about a specific topic.

While there are many variations of the technique (and it has applicability to other thought problems as well) the one I have found to be the most effective is as follows:

(1) *Become aware that your thoughts need stopping.*

(2) *Select an attractive alternative "thought project."* It is necessary to have two or three of these prepared in advance. "Thought projects" must be able to compete with the obsessive or bothersome thoughts and should, therefore, be of strong interest to the depressed person. Since it is not possible to stop *all* thinking, and since the thought energy needs to go somewhere, the competing alternative thought must be able to capture that energy.

The task of selecting alternative thought projects is central to this technique, so let me illustrate how I do this. When I learned to fly some years ago, I loved to replay in my mind all the flight procedures I had mastered, so I would mentally rehearse takeoffs and landings. If my mind was very active at night and I could not get to sleep, I would turn to this as a thought project. I would imagine I was preparing an airplane for flight, performing all the preflight checks, taxiing to the runway and making radio calls. Using this as a thought project was an effective way to rehearse the flying procedures I was learning, but at the same time it provided me with an attractive alternative toward which I could redirect my thoughts. I seldom got as far as takeoff before falling asleep.

It is possible to do the same thing with any project that interests you. Prayer, meditation, rehearsing New Testament Greek vocabulary, memorizing Scripture verses, or recalling the stories of your childhood are all potential thought projects that can redirect a person's thinking. It's wise to have several projects ready as alternatives in case the first one is not effective.

(3) *Take a minute to deliberately flood the mind with the obsessive negative thought.* This step is known as "paradoxical intention." It works on the principle that a troublesome thought is more likely to persist in a mind that is avoiding it than in one that welcomes it. When we deliberately force ourselves to think about the thought we want to avoid, the need for it subsides. By saturating our minds with the troublesome thought, we rob it of its power to create anxiety. Our minds can then more easily be turned in other directions. This is a powerful technique and, once mastered, can be used in many situations.

(4) *Now turn the mind in the direction of the new thought project and concentrate on it.*

As an example of the way thought stopping can work to keep us from emotional chaining, let us assume it is Sunday evening. Joe, a minister, has preached two or three times that day or taught a couple of adult classes, and he is unhappy about his effectiveness; he feels he has failed. Nothing went as planned. Joe's mind persists in rehearsing the events of the day and he can't let go of the troublesome thoughts.

At this point Joe realizes he is chaining and creating many secondary emotional reactions that have nothing to do with the original cause for his upset. Since he enjoys gardening, he has selected as his alternative thought project the planning and preparation of a new portion of his garden. So now he starts to "thought stop" by deliberately flooding his mind with the troublesome thoughts. He says to himself, "Now I'm going to think about my failure today. I'm going to rehearse all the events of the day and imprint them indelibly on my mind. Come on now, think about what happened—my stammering, poor choice of illustrations, irritation at the noisy kids in the front row. . . ." Joe forces himself to continue thinking about the events of the day for about a minute or two, and then he switches to thinking about his gardening project. If his mind goes back to the troublesome event, he repeats the flooding and switches again—to a new thought project, if necessary. Before he knows it, Joe is asleep, and his minor depression is gone within a day or two.

The steps outlined in this chapter for identifying the trigger of depression and preventing emotional chaining will not prevent all depression. But they can do much to avoid inappropriate depression and can help appropriate depression accomplish its purpose without being unnecessarily prolonged or perpetuated.

# 8

## THE PHASES OF DEPRESSION—
## MIDDLE STAGE

During the middle stage of a depression the deepest misery is experienced and the full impact of depression is felt. Not only is this the longest stage, but it is also the time when the symptoms reach their peak in severity. The depressed person typically feels that the suffering will never end. (This may be expressed as feelings of hopelessness about the future.)

Under this pressure a significant change in personality may occur and uncharacteristic behavior take place. The depressed person may say and do things he will regret afterwards. (However, depending on how severe the depression is, there is also a chance he may later lose his memory concerning some aspects of it.)

There are differences, of course, in the ways different individuals experience the middle stage of depression. Our discussion here will focus primarily on the long depressions, since they are the most difficult to handle. Depressions of short duration, lasting from a few hours to a few days or even weeks, are self-limiting and usually require little attention other than allowing oneself to grieve over the loss that triggered them.

### Factors That Can Cause Problems in the Middle Stage of Depression

Whether the depression is reactive or endogenous, the problems of the middle stage tend to be aggravated by the following:

(1) *Self-condemnation*. People who have high expectations for themselves (and this includes many ministers and Christian workers) often develop strong feelings of self-condemnation that accentuate depres-

sion. I have found that when a person openly admits that he is depressed and, without engaging in self-blame, accepts the experience as the inevitable consequence of his life circumstances, he can more easily and less painfully weather the storm. Fighting, denying, and resisting the depression only serve to aggravate and prolong it. Admittedly, a depressed person may not be able to completely avoid self-blame, since it is so much a part of the depression, but this is what he must strive for.

A person who has failed to come to terms with his humanness and fallibility will have great difficulty avoiding self-condemnation and therefore depression. I believe that much depression among ministers and Christians in general could be avoided if more of us developed a healthy "theology of failure." To do this, we must strive to set aside all misconceptions about being perfect and to more deeply understand the purpose of God's grace. We must repeatedly challenge the irrational idea that, if we fail at what we do, we are failures at the core of our being.

It is my conviction that many of us are, despite our evangelical soundness, too dependent on works for our sense of personal well-being. Too often our self-esteem is based on the belief that we are only worthy if we are capable and competent at everything we do. This is a product of our culture's performance mentality, which in many ways parallels the attitudes and beliefs of the Pharisees. Healthy self-esteem should be based on realistic self-knowledge, which implies that we know our weaknesses as well as our strengths and can accept both. (Weaknesses that can be changed should be changed, but those that cannot need to be accepted for what they are.) If we cannot accept imperfection, we will always fear failure. But if we accept our imperfection we will learn to be tolerant of our failure, to see it as inevitable and not as reflecting an inadequacy at the core of our being. We will therefore be better able to resist self-condemnation.

The tendency to allow failure to be destructive is so prevalent in our culture that many of us fail to realize things could be different. On the whole, we are not taught how to use failure constructively, and this cultural hang-up with performance as the criterion for personal well-being has carried over into our Christian communities. Life, including Christian service, was meant to be a trial-and-error learning process. In order to learn, we have to make mistakes as well as succeed. Failure is for growth; every failure should help prepare us to avoid the next one. But if we look at failure negatively, the learning process will be inhibited. We will be more likely to judge and condemn ourselves, and depression will be the likely result.

(2) *Guilt feelings*. Depression tends to increase feelings of guilt even

when in reality there is no basis for them. The guilt feelings accompanying depression are often misunderstood and they can, through the process of emotional chaining, give rise to a host of secondary reactions which compound the depression. Since the most moral of us can feel intense guilt for no reason when we are depressed, these feelings must simply be accepted as symptoms of the depression and not necessarily as convictions of the Holy Spirit.

Often it is the most strait-laced and uptight people who feel the guiltiest when they are depressed. These are people who have developed an inflexible value system, who see everything as being either good or bad. Depression undermines this defense mechanism, and the overly "moral" person finds that he cannot fit his feelings into his value system. Since in his mind everything that is not good is bad, he must be just that!

One way a depressed person can counter the excessive feelings of guilt that aggravate his depression is to learn to engage in positive self-talk to counter the negative self-condemnation. Counterstatements such as the following, used by a spouse or friend every time an expression of guilt is stated, can also help:

— "Your guilt is a product of your depression."
— "Whatever true guilt there is has been forgiven."
— "The fact that you *feel* guilty doesn't mean that you *are* guilty."
— "God understands that your guilt feelings are a product of your depression."

(3) *Boredom and spiritual emptiness*. While everybody gets bored with aspects of life, a normal boredom differs from that of depression in that it readily dissipates when some new challenge or activity comes along. The depressed person cannot shake off the boredom. For the Christian this boredom can be experienced as a spiritual emptiness. When a pastor, who is expected to minister to the spiritual needs of others, experiences this emptiness, the consequences can be serious.

For a pastor, a period of spiritual emptiness coupled with depression can perhaps best be handled by a leave of absence and intensive professional treatment for the depression. While this may represent some sacrifice, in the long run it can work to prevent a much greater loss. Let's face it: A church depends greatly on the leadership and spiritual fruit of the minister. Whether he or she is a senior pastor with all the preaching responsibilities, a pastor of evangelism, a youth minister, or a minister of music, a minister is expected to continuously give of himself or herself. This giving comes from spiritual experiences and resources from within, and these resources cannot be tapped when a person is depressed. Ministers are kindest to both their congregations and themselves if they take the time to rest. An athlete with a sprained ankle will rest and seek healing. A singer with an infected throat will rest and treat the infection. Why should the pastor who is experiencing a temporary period of emptiness not do the same?

If no leave of absence is possible, the appropriate treatment must still be sought; depressed ministers who persist in their work without treatment are being inconsiderate of themselves, their families, and the souls for which they have pastoral care. During the period of his treatment, the minister will need to be upheld with much prayer. His or her vulnerability to temptation and despair will be much greater during this period of reduced ability to utilize the spiritual resources of the gospel. The minister will need God's protection—and the expressed love and support of his family, friends, and congregation.

(4) *Anger.* Since depression and anger go hand in hand, it is common for depression-prone people also to be angry people. The anger shows itself in attitudes, in body language, in tone of voice. Sometimes it is expressed directly and actively. Other times it is repressed and finds expression in passive and indirect ways.

Whether the anger is given overt expression (ventilated) or swallowed (repressed) it can cause trouble. Directly expressed anger can cause confusion because it distorts communication and creates interpersonal conflict. Anger also tends to lead to self-pity, and as a result conflict can remain as a festering sore. But repressed anger tends to be even more dangerous. As Harry Stack Sullivan, the well-known psychiatrist, says, "swallowing too much anger will ruin one's belly"— repressed anger can cause physical complaints such as ulcers. It can also lead to negativity, resistance, pessimism, and sulking—passive maneuvers that can be as destructive of relationships as direct confrontations.

Such manifestations of anger are very common during the middle stage of depression because the resources for coping with conflict will be depleted. To survive without catastrophe, it is better for the depressed person to be open about his angry feelings and to literally force himself not to run away from troublesome situations.

Anger can be a special problem for a depressed minister because congregations tend not to handle conflict well. Probably the best tactic for a minister who is struggling with angry feelings is to select a few key people and take them into confidence, sharing with them the fact that he or she is experiencing a period of depression and doesn't have the resources to deal well with the anger. Such frank openness can be a healing experience for both the pastor and the people. I've known situations in which the pastor has done this and found that one of the persons in the sharing group was in a similar state of depression. The relief for both was a major factor in breaking a deadlock and aborting a potentially disastrous church crisis.

I do recommend, however, that such open sharing be restricted to a select group. The average church congregation is composed of such a variety of people that there are bound to be those who will not be able to accept the fact that the pastor can have a weakness and who may use the minister's honest admission in a destructive way. There may be some situations in which it is possible to be frank with the whole congregation, but much wisdom must be used in judging whether or not—and when—this should be done.

(5) *Fatigue and weakness.* One of the protective functions of depression is to conserve energy. Unfortunately, this diminished energy can be the source of much frustration, especially since it does not always improve with rest. To someone who is depressed, even the smallest tasks demand much effort, and simple, routine chores like shaving or getting dressed seem arduous. The frustrations of these moments can be so overwhelming that the depressed person bursts out crying. And this problem can be especially difficult for the minister, whose work includes responsibility for the work of many besides himself or herself.

There is no easy way to avoid the fatigue of depression. To some extent, its message must be heeded. Instead of fighting the tired feeling, it is a good idea for depressed persons to modify their work schedules and reduce the demands on their energy. An early afternoon nap, if it can be arranged, can be very helpful in avoiding the need to "crash" later in the day or evening.

However, while the feeling of fatigue should generally be heeded, it should not always be indulged. Unless some demand on the energy system is maintained, a state of chronic fatigue may set in. Striking a balance between heeding the signs of fatigue and resisting the tendency to be overwhelmed by tiredness is not easy, but it is necessary. A spouse may have to act as referee, forcing the depressed person to get out of bed when he feels like sleeping in, planning activities to keep him occupied, or ensuring that he keeps his appointments. When willpower won't work, it's often necessary to set up an external system of accountability to ensure that obligations are met.

(6) *Slowed thinking and poor memory.* Apart from the spiritual consequences of slowed thinking and unreliable memory, these byproducts of depression also impair work ability. Ministers may find that sermon preparation becomes difficult or perhaps impossible, and that they must rely more than usual on sermon notes. Many people find that recalling well-known facts, Scripture verses, or—more embarrassing—people's names is hard.

These memory difficulties are quite common, and the memory can be expected to return to normal when the depression passes. In the meantime, it's a good idea for the depressed person to use a notebook for jotting down points to remember and to rely on an appointment book for all engagements. There's no need to feel embarrassed about needing such memory aids; probably no one will even notice.

A depressed minister's inability to be creative in sermon preparation or program planning may be a more serious problem. The slowed thought processes may require more than usual stimulation to keep them functioning, so it is important to plan activities that will create interest, distract from the humdrum, and encourage creativity. A minister who is depressed may find it hard to take initiative in this planning and may have to depend on a spouse or friend to help him.

(7) *Delusions*. Peculiar or even bizarre thoughts may accompany a depression. Since these thoughts are foreign to the person's former thinking they can be very bothersome. They may take the form of obscene ideas, persistent fantasies, or irrational fears.

In less severe depressions, these distortions of thought can usually be easily recognized and appropriate adjustments made to discount them. The technique of thought stopping, which we have already discussed, can be helpful in doing this. In very severe depressions, however, foreign or strange thoughts cannot easily be countered. They can become firmly entrenched and may even be acted upon by the depressed person. When such distorted thoughts become fixed as beliefs, they are referred to as "delusions."

Reasoning with a person who suffers from delusions doesn't always work because they are sometimes caused by chemical imbalances in the brain. I have known wives to waste many hours trying to convince a depressed husband that his thoughts and fears had no truth in them. Sometimes the depressed person seems to derive satisfaction from other people's attempts to argue with their delusions, but he may also become frightened when his delusional orientations are attacked and may therefore become alienated from other people. In general, challenging the delusional beliefs of a severely depressed person only unnerves him and creates insecurity. But this does not mean he should be allowed to act on the basis of his delusions. The family of such an individual should always be on the alert and ready to intervene if any sign is given of acting out the delusion.

## The Possibility of Suicide

During the middle stage of depression, the severely depressed person may become so miserable that he will try anything to ease his mental and emotional pain. He may withdraw from all social contacts or attempt to escape from the realities of life by resorting to alcohol and drugs. He may also attempt suicide.

Since depression occurs at all ages and in all types of people, the possibility of suicide must always be kept in mind, no matter how unlikely the candidate. Children and adolescents as well as adults and the elderly, can be tempted to take drastic steps to end the misery of depression.

To an alarming degree, more and more people are taking this way out of their depression, presumably because suicide has come to have less of a social stigma attached to it, and because the means for accomplishing it easily (drugs, for instance) are now more readily available. What is especially alarming is that more and more Christians now seem to find it an option worth considering. Ministers, helping professionals, and their families are not exempt from the risk of suicide. Because this is true, I think it is important to include a look at suicide in our discussion of the middle stage of depression.

At the outset, however, I want to stress that while every depressed person probably *thinks about* escaping through death, and may even be preoccupied with the idea, not everyone actually resorts to suicide. And there is little reason to fear that broaching the subject of suicide will "give the depressed person the idea." In fact, the risk of suicide is more likely to be increased when those closest to the depressed person refrain from mentioning the subject. In most cases the depressed person *wants* to talk about his death thoughts and finds it helpful to share them. When this is not possible, there may be an increased urge to try the act itself. And even suicide attempts that are only half-hearted and inadequately performed can sometimes succeed and actually result in death. Any threat of suicide, therefore, must *always* be taken seriously.

## Myths about Suicide

There are many myths surrounding suicide. These misconceptions can mislead the sufferer as well as those close to him, thus preventing early recognition of potential suicide. Common among the myths are:

(1) *If a person threatens suicide he won't carry it out.* NOT TRUE. A threat of suicide must always be taken seriously. Otherwise the one making the threat may follow through just out of pride or to prove a point.

(2) *Suicide threats are just a way of getting attention and manipulating people.* NOT ALWAYS. While some attempts at suicide are a way of gaining attention, many are not. And even a person crying for attention may actually kill himself. The "cry for help" contained even in the most blatantly manipulative threat must be heeded.

(3) *Someone who has attempted suicide once won't try it again.* NOT TRUE. Most successful suicides have been preceded by at least one previous attempt.

(4) *Deeply religious persons will not kill themselves.* NOT TRUE. Ministers, priests, and rabbis suffering from depression can take their own lives as readily as nonreligious persons. Beliefs and values, no matter how sincerely held, sometimes cannot override the powerful forces of depression.

## Recognizing Suicidal Tendencies

There is no way to absolutely predict a suicide; it can occur without warning. Many suicides, however, are preceded by warning signs that can be recognized and may serve to alert close friends and relatives:

(1) *The high-risk person will usually have experienced a significant recent loss that he or she believes cannot be replaced.* The loss may be concrete or abstract, real or imagined. The "irreplaceability" of the loss is the central risk factor, but since it is difficult to fully evaluate this, it is easy to misjudge this factor. The only way to know whether a loss is being perceived as irreplaceable or not is to ask and then to listen carefully to what is being said and also to what is not. The hidden messages of body language and behavior can often tell more than words.

(2) *In the high-risk person, an intense hostility usually accompanies the loss.* The anger may be directed toward the lost object or toward the cause of the loss. It is when this anger becomes directed toward the self that it can lead to suicide as self-punishment or as punishment of those who have caused the loss. The suicidal person often believes that he is getting even by taking his life and that those left behind will "feel sorry" for what they have done to cause the loss.

(3) *A series of disasters or a period of intense stress and fatigue before or following the loss may increase the risk of suicide.* These conditions disturb physical functioning and produce distortion of the emotions. Events are then more easily misinterpreted and defense mechanisms do not function normally.

(4) *Losses that cause extreme embarrassment and loss of face or that leave the individual feeling totally abandoned are more likely to provoke suicide than other forms of loss.*

(5) *A history of repeated depression and/or previous suicidal attempts must always be taken as a danger sign.* Suicide becomes easier with practice. Repeated depression creates an attitude of lost hope and a feeling of futility about the future.

(6) *Of all the warning signs of impending suicide the one to watch for is increased "secretiveness."* While not all suicides are carefully planned beforehand, many are. The elaborate planning that goes into the preparation is often relished by the depressed person who may, for

example, lock himself in his room, rummage through old drug bottles, claim insomnia, ask for prescription sleeping pills, or give other such clues to his intentions. Any secretive or unusual behavior by a severely depressed person should be carefully checked out and confronted boldly and assertively.

## Helping the Person Who Is Contemplating Suicide

The primary goal of all help must be to encourage the person contemplating suicide to reconsider his or her actions, explore alternatives, and find resources for help. Speed of intervention, reversal of the despair, reduction of hostility, and reawakening of hope are all essential if suicide is to be prevented. To do this, it is necessary to be frank. The topic needs to be brought out in the open and the depressed person explicitly encouraged to talk about his suicidal thoughts. Avoidance of the topic is dangerous.

Frequently it is not enough to be supportive; it may be necessary to take assertive action, to tell the depressed person what he must do and how he must do it. While nondirective support is helpful in other types of depression, when suicide is a danger it is essential that the depressed person not be left alone. If necessary, a stay in the hospital, where continuous observation can take place, may be necessary. A doctor, a psychologist, or a psychiatrist can be consulted for advice on how to implement this. Of course, the depressed person can't be expected to be very cooperative at this point—strong coercion may be needed.

Perhaps the most helpful step of all is facilitating the reduction of anger toward the lost object or toward those perceived as causing the loss. The idea is to get the person to talk about his anger, to experience it, and to ventilate the hostile feelings. Within reasonable limits almost anything that facilitates this is acceptable. The helper can encourage these expressions of anger by being an effective and participative listener. Again, there is little danger that suicide will be encouraged or the depression aggravated by this process. Quite the reverse is true. Talking about these feelings can bring a new perspective and help to clarify issues concerning the underlying loss. Even if the anger is transformed into more depression, the grieving process will be helped and the risk of suicide diminished.

Here are two final words about suicide and depression:

(1) *No one should ever try to deal with a potential suicide alone.* A depressed person contemplating suicide or the family and friends of such a sufferer should always seek expert help.

(2) *There are some who are so determined to take their lives that nothing can be done to prevent it.* As a psychotherapist I have had a

few such patients. It is extremely important for the family, friends, or counselors of someone who has succeeded in taking his or her life, NOT TO BLAME THEMSELVES. With the best skill in the world they still may not have been able to prevent it from happening. Life is just too painful for some people, and nothing will deter them from taking the ultimate way out.

## Facilitating the Middle Stage of Depression

While it is important to be informed about suicide, it is also important to be aware that most depressions do not result in or even threaten suicide. The middle stage of depression is usually self-limiting when left to itself, and even a severe depression will eventually lift. The middle stage of a depression can be helped by the following four steps, which should be implemented in dependence on God's Spirit to facilitate the healing process.

(1) *The tendency to feed the depression by the creation of additional losses through emotional or cognitive chaining must be prevented.* The middle stage is prone to perpetuation through chaining. (Abusing the body and mental systems through fatigue, stress, alcohol, or drugs can aggravate this tendency.)

Typically, depressed persons begin to appraise the experience and symptoms in a negative way. They misinterpret their feelings as signals of defeat, failure, hopelessness, and deprivation. Everything appears deficient, inadequate, unworthy, or unpleasant to them, and they attribute blame for all this to themselves.

For example, a pastor may believe that his preaching is absolutely worthless and feel sure that nobody benefits from anything he says. He may delve through old sermons to find a previous "hit" and, with minor modifications, preach it in the hope that he can recover his confidence. But then he may continue to feed his depression by interpreting every reaction of his congregation as negative and rejecting. (Even *positive* feedback may be distorted and interpreted as criticism.) The depressed minister may anticipate failure and then set about making sure it happens. Then, when he does fail, he blames himself and becomes even more self-critical, activating more feelings of loss and intensifying the depression even more.

Experimental studies have shown, however, that except in very severe depressions a depressed person *can* be helped to recognize how he distorts his experiences, and this can cut down on such emotional chaining. Self-criticism, self-condemnation, and pessimism cannot be entirely removed, since they are a product of the depression, but they can be reduced. The sufferer can be helped to distrust his distorted perceptions, to say to himself, "I know that I see things negatively but this is not how the world really is; it's a function of my depressed state. Therefore, during this period of time I won't trust my feelings but I'll do what I *think* is correct." Doing this will not take away the depression, but it can help prevent the triggering of further depression.

Friends, family, and counselors can help the depressed person learn to distrust his distorted perceptions by continually challenging the distortions and giving him positive and realistic feedback. Since depressed people are often resistant to taking advice, this may take persistence; a stone can't be eroded with one or two drops of water. But once a beginning is made in eroding the negative thoughts, the downward spiral of the depression will have been halted and healing can begin.

(2) *Where a legitimate loss has occurred, the process of grieving must be fully implemented;* the depressed person must be given every opportunity to mourn the loss. Such grief, when it is allowed, is normal, natural, and self-limiting. It can help for close friends and relatives to give clear "permission" for the depressed person to grieve. This can be done either verbally or by an attitude of acceptance. If a person who has suffered the loss wants to be alone, avoid responsibility, and back down from previous commitments, this should be allowed; grieving cannot take place in the midst of activity. The right attitude of acceptance and unconditional love—observing the wishes of the sufferer, giving him "space" if he wants it, refraining from pressuring him—can make the difference between a "normal" depression and one that will be painfully prolonged.

It is particularly important to reassure the sufferer that the depression is not outside God's will for him or her, that it is not a sign of failure or of God's rejection. Scripture, especially the Psalms, can be a rich source of reassurance for depressed persons.

(3) *The reality of the loss must be confronted and accepted.* No reactive depression can be completed until the reality of the loss is fully realized and accepted. One of the reasons a concrete loss is easier to cope with is that we are usually forced to accept the loss more definitely. The immediate depressive response may be more painful, but this deeper experience of depression brings quicker healing. Abstract and threatened losses are harder to grieve over because they are more elusive.

Sometimes the process of grieving must be aided by forcing the affected person to confront and accept the reality of the loss. (If no actual loss has taken place, then the realization of this should end the depressive process.) Forcing someone to confront the reality of a loss may at first seem cruel and callous—and, of course, it should be done with kindness and sensitivity. But loss has to be faced realistically before the depression can be completed and healing begin. All of us have a strong tendency to engage in denial, to indulge in fantasies about "what might have been" if a loss had not taken place. But such denial, self-pity, and wasted thought only serve to keep us from completing the grieving process and recovering from the depression.

(4) *A new perspective on the loss must emerge before the depression can abate.* This step—placing the loss in proper perspective—both accompanies and follows step 3. As a depressed person is forced to accept the reality of a loss and to say, in effect, "It's gone! It's never coming back. That is the end of this prized object, job, or person," he also needs to begin to place the loss in the perspective of larger life issues. In other words, he must eventually go on to say, "But this is not the end of everything. There will be other objects and persons to prize."

Most of us tend to exaggerate loss, to convince ourselves that the things we love are irreplaceable. And it is true that some things cannot be replaced exactly as before, but we can often find reasonable substitutes for many things we care about. And in situations where what we lose cannot be replaced—for instance, when a loved one dies—we must still eventually accept the loss and go on with life.

This is why we need perspective on the larger issues of existence. One reason I prize my Christian faith so much is that it gives me that kind of perspective, even about very severe losses. It provides an overall way of looking at things that makes it easier to fit the smaller pieces into the puzzle. The perspective on life that God gives through faith in Christ can make the difference between whether we see loss as catastrophic or not. Our attitudes toward money, possessions, accomplishments, and ambitions are influenced by our faith—or at least they should be! God's values become our values if we stay close to him.

I am not suggesting that this automatically prevents us from becoming depressed whenever we experience loss. After all, God made us in such a way that we respond to loss by grieving over it. But I do believe that the perspective faith gives us can help facilitate the process of healing by eventually helping us put the loss in proper perspective.

Without faith in God I cannot imagine how anyone comes to terms with life! I am extremely impressed by the apostle Paul's way of dealing with loss. In Philippians 3:7–8 he says, "But what things were gain to me, those I counted loss for Christ. Yea doubtless, and I count all things but loss for the excellency of the knowledge of Christ Jesus my Lord: for whom I have suffered the loss of all things."

I find this verse very helpful in showing how I can keep my losses in perspective. First, I can prepare myself for the losses of life before they happen by "counting" them as loss. The term *counting* refers to a process of modifying beliefs and attitudes. By sorting out my values in the context of my Christian faith, I can develop a new perspective on loss before the loss occurs and thus reduce the severity of the depression which follows—or eliminate it altogether. This step is *preventive*.

When I am actually confronted by a significant loss, the value I place on the knowledge of Christ Jesus as my Lord can help me place the loss in proper perspective. Then, since everything I want outside of him is of lesser importance, I can more quickly and effectively see my loss for what it is. In effect, I place what I have lost alongside everything I have gained in Christ—and its value seems to fade, just as a candle loses its brightness when placed beside the sun. This step is *therapeutic*.

# 9

# THE PHASES OF DEPRESSION—
# RECOVERY

Transition from the middle to the recovery stage of depression is not usually accompanied by any dramatic sign; it happens subtly and very gradually. In the milder depressions, the recovery may be more noticeable because it occurs so rapidly. In the severe, lengthy depressions, especially of the endogenous type, the recovery takes place very slowly and the turning point is usually not obvious until the sufferer is well into the recovery.

As a general rule, provided there is no extraordinary factor operating to produce relapse or prolongation of the depression, one can say that the longer the depression, the more difficult it will be to identify the beginning of recovery and the slower will be the rate of recovery. Much of what we will discuss here relates to the serious depressions of long duration, since depressions of short duration seldom present problems during the recovery phase.

## The Importance of Recognizing the Recovery Phase

Even though it is often difficult to pinpoint the beginning of the recovery, it is important that this be attempted for three reasons: (1) The strategy for treating the depression changes when recovery begins; (2) the potential for creating further depression may temporarily increase; and (3) the risk of suicide may also temporarily increase at this time.

During the recovery phase the depressed person will begin to have moments when he feels better. These moments may occur at unexpected times and may not always be related to what is happening in the environment. While these "normal" periods may bring some relief to the sufferer, they have the unfortunate effect of accentuating the low mood when it returns. It is not unlike what happens when our eyes have adjusted to a dimly lit room. If someone temporarily switches on a bright light and then returns the room to darkness, it may appear to be darker than it really is.

Another way of illustrating the phenomenon is to remember that valleys seem deeper when mountains are higher. Returning to depression after a period of normal feelings or even feelings of elation makes everything seem gloomier than before. As a result, the sufferer may fear that the depression is getting worse or that it will never pass.

It is during such a time that further depression may be triggered. The person may feel acute despair and may even resort to suicide. Since both these consequences are due to misinterpreting the variations of mood occuring during the recovery phase, it is essential that the sufferer be prepared to receive these fluctuations for what they are— namely a sign that the depression is lifting. He or she must understand that the apparent increase in the low mood is due entirely to the juxtaposition of a moment of normality with the ongoing depression. The contrast makes the depression seem deeper.

## Signs that Recovery Is Beginning

One of the earliest signs that a depression is beginning to pass, and the one I most frequently look for, is the fact that these *moments of normality come more often*. As in a storm that is beginning to clear, moments of sunshine will break through the thick clouds. Here and there, just for a moment, the sun will begin to shine again.

These first glimpses of normality will often not be trusted by the depressed person and can easily go unnoticed. Then gradually, as the depression begins to pass and these moments of sunshine become more frequent, the sufferer will begin to acknowledge that the depression is lifting.

A second sign of recovery is that the depressed person reports being able to think more clearly. While the low mood may still be present, problems which characterized the middle stage begin to abate. Memory improves; appointments are not forgotten so readily. Concentration becomes easier and the "fog" which permeated all previous thinking becomes only a light mist.

Finally, the person begins to report more normal periods than periods of depression. There is a danger at this point in the case of an endogenous depression that is being treated with anti-depressant medication. Because the symptoms are not so severe at this point the patient may develop a false sense of well-being and prematurely stop the treatment. This increases the risk of relapse. Treatment needs to be continued through the recovery stage, and well beyond the period when the depression seems to be gone. The general rule is that anti-depressant medication should be continued three to six months after the end of a severe depression of the endogenous type.

## Problems of the Recovery Stage

The problems encountered during the recovery stage can be grouped into two categories:

(1) *Those which are the direct consequences of the depression process.* The biochemistry of the recovery stage is not understood any better than the biochemistry of depression itself. Presumably, what happens is that the physiological process causing the depression begins to return the body and mind to normal functioning. It is a *process*, however; it does not occur all at once, although in the minor depressions where the body chemistry has only been slightly disturbed recovery may appear to be instantaneous.

The fact that recovery is a gradual process must be emphasized to the depressed person. I can recall one minister who would not accept this. He was by nature impulsive and impatient. He would not accept the fact that recovery takes time, and he became very angry with me for not producing an "instant cure." The result was that he prolonged his depression well beyond the point of expected recovery, because he was demanding more of himself and his physiology than was reasonable. This is like demanding on instant cure for influenza. The expectation that one can recover rapidly from a deep depression is just as unreasonable and will only create further frustration and depression.

(2) *Those resulting from the habits and behavior patterns learned or acquired during the depression.* This second category is by far the most difficult to deal with. The habits and behavior patterns established during a depression take their toll during the recovery phase. The truth of the matter is that, while depression produces a lot of misery for the sufferer, it also pays many dividends. Some people actually enjoy their depression, or at least they give that impression.

I use the term *enjoy* here to denote a certain type of satisfaction that many sufferers feel despite their misery. Their depression relieves them of many responsibilities. They receive a lot of sympathetic understanding, and previously hostile people may now even become friendly. While the depressed person would not consciously seek these "secondary gains," the fact that they naturally occur leads to their easy and unquestioned acceptance. Who is going to look a gift horse in the mouth? Who would not, when in a depressed state, find relief by avoiding decisions or responsibilities?

But these benefits can begin to change a person's personality. It is very easy for new habits to become formed. Persons who were extremely active and conscientious may, after a serious depression, find that out of habit they prefer to sit around and do nothing. Enthusiasm only brings responsibility, so why show any enthusiasm? They may unconsciously develop a preference for an easygoing, low-pressured existence. To some extent this may not be so bad, as most of us need to learn how to live at a more leisurely pace. Often, however, the pendulum will swing too far over to a preference for inactivity. Striking a balance by breaking lazy habit patterns is a necessary step during the recovery stage.

To return to a well-balanced work attitude, people who are recovering from depression must first understand and accept that the predisposition to maintaining a low-energy level is a product of the habits learned during the depression. Spouses and close friends can frequently remind them of this while encouraging them to begin extending themselves, taking on more responsibility, and returning to a normal level of activity. It doesn't work to wait for energetic feelings before taking on activity; persons recovering from depression must begin to behave energetically even though they do not feel like it. The feeling will follow later.

Another set of habits which may become established during a depression has to do with the unconscious rewards of manipulation. Often a depressed person learns that he or she can control his or her environment quite effectively by "turning on" the depression. This makes others quite naturally feel sympathetic. They will be cautious in what they do and say, how they respond to the depressed person's ideas or requests. People are so much nicer to someone who is depressed, and a person who has previously not been able to get his or her way may quite suddenly discover that depression confers a tremendous amount of power. After many months of having this power to manipulate and to obtain love from others, the recovering person may have trouble giving it up. Quite unintentionally, he may fall into the habit of putting on a display of depression to obtain some personal advantage over a spouse, friend, or co-worker.

One church worker who used this tactic rather excessively during a recovery phase found it nearly cost him his marriage and his church position. As his depression began to lift, his wife reduced the number of things she would do for him so as to provide encouragement for him to resume normal activity. She was employed in a professional position and, since their children had left home, her husband shared many household chores with her. She would prepare breakfast and then go to work, leaving him to take care of the dishes. During his depression she had taken over his chores because his condition had barely allowed him to perform his essential pastoral duties. This had helped to conserve his energy for essential work. But once recovery had begun his wife asked if he would resume taking care of the morning dishes as before.

At this point the pastor's depression appeared to worsen. She would awaken him, take her shower, and return to find that he was still in bed. After further prompting he would reluctantly get out of bed, complaining about how terrible he felt. She would leave for work and, upon returning in the early afternoon, find him still in bed. This infuriated her. She knew he was manipulating her into continuing the pattern of duties established during the depression. Her reaction prompted some legitimate further depression in the pastor, but fortunately it was of short duration and a satisfactory solution was eventually worked out.

Such crisis episodes, in which habits acquired during a depression are used to manipulate others, are very common during the recovery phase. With careful preparation, a clear understanding of the dynamics of recovery, and loving confrontation, these episodes can be avoided or turned to good advantage.

## Facilitating the Recovery Phase

There are five ways the recovery phase can be facilitated:

(1) *Increase physical activity.* I have already alluded to the fact that many depressions show remarkable improvement following increased physical activity. But while physical exercise can be helpful at any stage of a depression, it is not always possible to motivate patients to do exercise at earlier stages. The depression makes them feel lethargic and robs them of energy. During the recovery phase the ability to engage in physical exercise begins to return, although they may still not feel very enthusiastic.

To overcome this reluctance it may be helpful to arrange outings that require some physical effort, or plan some activity such as gardening or house painting that will demand physical involvement. Or the recovering person can be enrolled in a gym club. (Every city has a YMCA that provides, at a very reasonable cost, a wide range of physical activities.) Whatever tactic is used, the objective is simple: increase physical output.

One minister I treated for depression had been an excellent swimmer in his high school days. During the early years of his work he had forgotten how good a swimmer he was and how much enjoyment it gave him. I encouraged him to join the local YMCA where there is a heated indoor swimming pool. He quickly recovered his swimming skills and established a regular habit of exercise. Not only did this speed up his recovery, but it also provided him an opportunity to spend time with his two sons, aged ten and eight, who were able to develop some of their own natural swimming talent.

There are many other ways to increase physical activity. Walking each evening, purchasing a bicycle exerciser and placing it in front of the television set (making a rule that the news or other favored TV program can only be watched if the exerciser is being used), forming a jogging club at the church, or learning a new sport can all speed recovery from depression as well as provide many other benefits.

(2) *Assume increased responsibilities.* A severe depression inevitably requires some cutting back of responsibilities. It is a rare individual who can continue to function at full effectiveness under the cloud of an affective disorder. During the recovery phase, a gradual return to fulfilling former responsibilities should take place. There will be a natural resistance to this due to the remaining lethargy, feelings of inadequacy, and fear that a relapse may occur. Often those who are recovering from depression will feel uncertain about their competence and will lack self-confidence. But such feelings need not dictate actions. It is important that recovering persons force themselves not to trust their feelings of inadequacy—to say to themselves, "The fact that I *feel* inadequate doesn't mean that I *am* inadequate," then to take the plunge into some task needing attention. Feelings of confidence can be expected to return *after* the task has been accomplished successfully. (Of course, it would be self-destructive for any recovering person to "take the plunge" on some mammoth task which has a high risk for failure. It is wiser to begin with relatively "safe" and easy-to-complete chores, then progress gradually to more demanding tasks.)

In the early part of the recovery phase it can be helpful for recovering persons to structure their day's work around a preplanned schedule. The advantages are twofold. First, their memory may not yet be functioning effectively, and the schedule will help with keeping appointments or fulfilling obligations. Second, it is extremely important that people recovering from depression feel a sense of closure and accomplishment at the end of a day. A carefully worked-out schedule does this by giving a clear picture of what has been done in a given day.

Of course, in order for a schedule to work this way, the amount of work planned for each day must be *reasonable* and *realistic*. Those who don't succeed with their first day's goals need to reduce the planned workload for the next day to the point that they are confident they can accomplish it. It is important to keep adjusting the planned goals until a reasonable balance is reached, because either overestimating or underestimating the amount that can be accomplished will only provoke disappointment and further depression.

(3) *Change inner self-statements.* During a bout with depression many irrational ideas become established. These may emerge as negative or erroneous "self-talk"—statements the depressed person makes to himself *about* himself. Since such ideas are the product of the distorted perceptions of the depression, they normally diminish as the depression passes, but not always. Sometimes they can become deeply entrenched in the belief or attitudinal systems and will need attention.

For example, a depressed minister's idea that he or she will never recover from depression will fade as recovery progresses. The fear that the depression will cause church members to mistrust the minister's judgment is more likely to remain. If a recovering minister persists in dwelling on this fear, he or she will very soon begin behaving as if it were true. And this irrational, paranoid behavior, in turn, is apt to make the congregation uneasy and thus make the idea come true. This is how many self-fulfilling prophecies operate!

One way of dealing with irrational self-talk in the recovery phase of depression is to write the thoughts down. On paper they can be more easily recognized for what they are. Since irrational thinking is not always obvious to the depressed or recovering person, it's a good idea to ask a friend or counselor to look at the list of ideas and comment on them. A debate may even be necessary to reinforce the realization that these ideas have no basis in reality and that they are figments of the imagination, products of depression.

Actually, it can be helpful for all of us, depressed or not, to develop the habit of challenging our self-talk. This involves attacking our illogical ideas and replacing them with more realistic ones. It is easy to reach the point that we believe everything we say to ourselves, so we need to pray for God's Spirit to reveal to us how we distort events, think unclearly, or reason illogically.

For instance, if a minister finds himself thinking, "I did a terrible job of preaching today; I can never face my congregation again," he can then challenge this self-statement by saying, "Wait a moment! By whose judgment was it so terrible? What law says I must always feel good after I preach? How can I question how God will use my message?" Challenging his negative self-statement can help him keep his perspective and realistically assess his preaching, making changes if necessary and trusting God for the outcome of his efforts.

Destructive self-talk always has the following two characteristics: (1) The statements are made in absolute terms, and (2) blame is always attributed to oneself. The excessive use of absolutes in irrational self-talk takes the form of seeing everything in extremes: good and bad, perfect and imperfect, right and wrong, success and failure. No allowance is made for the grey areas of life. Accompanying the use of absolutes is the tendency to self-blame. The typical thought sequence is: "I failed at this task. I am therefore to blame for my failure. If I am to blame, then I must be worthless."

Such thoughts *must* be challenged. Leaving them in the head without questioning them is like leaving a cancerous tumor in the body. They can control feelings and behavior if left alone—no matter how ridiculous they are. Challenging the preceding thought sequence would involve saying to oneself, "Perhaps I did no wrong. Humans often make mistakes. I am a human and therefore cannot always be perfect. Let me now examine exactly what went wrong so I can try to correct it the next time."

On the matter of self-blame, let me make a further observation. When we are confronted by a failure, we tend not to distinguish between *responsibility* and *blame*. But there is an important difference between taking responsibility for your failure and taking blame for it. Responsibility is essentially constructive, but blame is destructive. Blaming implies judgment and condemnation and leads to self-punishment. Taking responsibility implies having a desire to correct the defective behavior as efficiently and expeditiously as possible without feeding feelings of inadequacy. Blaming confuses our imperfect acts with our sinful essence, whereas responsibility keeps them separate. As Christians, we live under the benefits of the Cross, and it is therefore theologically inappropriate for us to blame ourselves in the way I have just described. To blame ourselves is to punish ourselves and deny the saving work of the Cross. It is more sound theologically to accept responsibility for failure and, where appropriate, to claim forgiveness.

(4) *Avoid depression-producing circumstances.* During recovery a depressed person's inner resources for coping with stress and loss will be depleted. This is not, therefore, the time to be exposed to high-risk situations. What is needed is a balance between assuming former responsibilities and avoiding situations that provoke frustration. If a pastor feels she can resume preaching responsibilities but cannot face the pressures of a counseling session or deacon's meeting, the thing for her to do is take on the former and ask to be excused from the latter. If another church worker feels he can reach out to people on an individual basis but cannot face large groups, then he needs to go ahead with what he feels is safe and comfortable. Some risk-taking will be necessary to obtain gratification and regain confidence, but the risks must be tailored to the level of improvement.

A number of changes may have to be made to avoid depression-producing situations:

—Modifying expectations and developing realistic goals.

—Reducing expectations of others. (When the depressed person grants others the privilege of being human, he lessens his disappointment when they fail and let him down.)

—Learning to be more decisive and to feel confident with decisions that have been made so as to reduce feelings of helplessness.

—Changing the motive behind ministry from working for recognition or to make up for a deficient ego to working for the glory of God.

—Learning to be more assertive in order to deal with frustrating people and to handle conflicts more constructively. (This can help the depressed person avoid the anger and inner rage that come from not knowing how to defend himself or stand up for his rights.)

During the recovery stage it is also important that you be self-forgiving and self-loving. By "self-loving" I mean being kind, patient, longsuffering, and gentle toward oneself; 1 Corinthians 13 is as applicable to self-love as it is to loving others.

(5) *Resume spiritual exercises.* As mentioned earlier, a hunger for God and his word is often diminished during a depression. This suppression of spiritual appetite is quite natural and bears no relation to one's spiritual standing; it must be accepted as a normal consequence of the depressed physical and mental state of the disorder. With recovery, however, interest in spiritual matters usually returns. There may be spontaneous bursts of interest in the reading of Scripture, prayer, and praise; these signs herald the return of normality. Unfortunately, however, the positive habits and disciplines which existed prior to the depression may have been undermined and it may now be necessary to set about reestablishing these habits of discipline and self-control. No Christian can function effectively in spiritual matters if he is not disciplined.

Good spiritual discipline, like good study habits, has to be developed. It doesn't come about naturally in most of us. What are its basic ingredients? I believe that, among other things, the following fundamental behaviors must be learned in order to accomplish self-control:

—*Delaying gratification* of immediate urges and pleasures in order to concentrate on the task at hand.

—*Resisting distraction* by sounds, events, interests, or activities that intrude on study time and prayer.

—*Prioritizing time and energy* so that more important tasks are accomplished first and less important tasks delayed until a more appropriate time.

—*Keeping short-term goals and long-term goals* in perspective so as to avoid being distracted by unnecessary, wasteful, and time-consuming trivialities.

Because it is extremely difficult when just coming out of a depression to reestablish self-discipline and restore previous good study and spiritual-development habits, some strategy may be needed to modify one's behavior. One tactic I recommend is establishing accountability with a spouse, close friend, or colleague. This is important because willpower alone simply can't be trusted to restore the needed discipline. Having someone to report to on a regular basis, however, can provide reinforcement for reestablishing old behaviors and for taking responsibility to accomplish goals. Establishing accountability can be a reciprocal practice; each person can monitor the other's progress in each of the behaviors mentioned above and hold him responsible for successes and failures. There is hardly any person—depressed or not—who would not benefit from some improvement in their study and spiritual habits.

# 10

## PROFESSIONAL TREATMENT OF DEPRESSION

Despite the progress in the understanding of emotional problems which has taken place during the past twenty years, there is still a strong general resistance to psychological or psychiatric treatment. Stereotyping and stigmatizing still prevail—as does the belief that people should be able to solve their own personal problems without outside help. This is especially true in Christian circles.

Quite apart from cultural stereotypes and beliefs, there has been, historically, a conflict between the mental-health professions and the Christian church which has produced much suspicion on both sides. Sigmund Freud is still an ogre to many devout Christians, and his influence in alienating the theological world from the healing professions is only now beginning to wane.

But Freud is not alone in provoking the suspicions of Christians toward the mental-health professions. Many contemporary systems of psychotherapy are, in my view, incompatible with a Christian view of life, and those that *are* basically compatible are frequently put into practice by people who are fundamentally distrustful of or hostile to the Christian faith. In fact, one of the best-known proponents of the particular psychological orientation I espouse is overtly atheistic. While he has willingly taken part in symposiums on religion at professional meetings, he openly criticizes many Christian ideas as leading to unnecessary guilt and even neurosis.

It is understandable, then, that there is tension and misunderstanding between Christians and the mental-health professions in general. I feel this is unfortunate. I believe there is an important place for Christian psychotherapy that makes use of the insights of modern psychology without distorting or denying the reality of Christian faith.

It is my strong belief that Christian conversion has saved more people from ruination, suicide, drug addiction, alcoholism, resentment, and anger than any system of psychiatric or psychological treatment I know. And it is my experience that inappropriate guilt or neuroses that seem to result from Christian faith are actually caused by distortions and misunderstandings on the part of sinful human beings. But this does not mean that every problem of the mind or the emotions can automatically be healed by conversion. It is one thing for the gospel to have the power to heal, it is another for persons to be able to appropriate this power. In other words, the problem is not with the gospel, but with people!

Often, emotional problems have their roots in early childhood experiences or in a disturbed physiology, and the help that the mental-health professions can offer—especially if integrated with a Christian view of life—can greatly facilitate the work of the gospel and unleash its resources for healing. God has provided us with a gospel that fits our needs; I marvel at its power and potential. But I also know how human beings operate. And I believe Christian psychotherapy can be extremely valuable in preparing people to receive the power of God, to allow the Holy Spirit to do his work, and to remove all encumbrances to fully realizing their potential as children of God.

## Christian Faith and Psychotherapy

How then should Christians view the mental-health professions and its tools—psychotherapy, psychiatry, and medicine—as they apply to mental and emotional problems? Since a correct attitude toward these issues is essential to the effectiveness of treatment for depression, allow me to make a few general comments which may clarify some of these issues:

(1) *While many philosophical assumptions underlying the systems of mental treatment available today are generally incompatible with a Christian world view, specific techniques, taken out of the context of their philosophical assumptions, can still be powerful in bringing healing.* An example would be the use of "behavior modification" to help a compulsive overeater. The philosophical ideas of behaviorism do not in all respects match a Christian world view. However, it is possible to set aside the philosophical assumptions and still use the method to treat a problem. This is no different than setting aside the beliefs of a research surgeon when using his technique for open-heart surgery.

It should be remembered that the person is the common denominator in all treatment approaches. Because of this, effective forms of treatment will always transcend the philosophical ideas of their originators, even though these originators may insist that the effectiveness of specific techniques prove the correctness of the philosophical system. Because it is possible to accept the technique without adopting the philosophy behind it, Christian therapists are free to utilize a wide variety of healing resources. The discoveries of psychotherapy are ultimately a product of God's intelligent creation anyway. A B. F. Skinner (the main developer of the techniques of behavior modification) can discover a system of stimulus-response mechanisms that can produce changes in behavior only because that is how God created organisms to operate. It is *not* Skinner's system, but God's. So we can feel free to use it without sacrificing the fundamental beliefs of our Christian point of view.

(2) *In seeking therapeutic help for mental and emotional problems, it is far more important to evaluate the personal characteristics of a specific psychotherapist or psychiatrist than to make sure his or her system of therapy conforms to a given world view.* Theologically sound Christian professionals come from backgrounds in many, if not all, of the theoretical systems. By far the majority of them are known as "eclectic," which means that while they may emphasize a particular point of view they also draw on a variety of specific techniques and match these to the particular problems or types of patients. It is the individual professional who primarily influences the therapy process.

(3) *Most of the more serious emotional problems have both an organic and a psychological basis and the most effective treatment may involve a combination of medical and psychological methods.* Evidence for this is growing rapidly. The skill needed to evaluate a specific problem and determine whether its cause is purely psychological, purely physiological, or perhaps a combination of the two is a skill that is independent of a particular belief system. This should encourage many ministers and Christians to seek professional help, if only for this initial evaluation. While I advocate that purely psychological problems be treated by a psychotherapist who will not undermine the Christian believer's faith system, the professional skills that must be utilized to unravel complex emotional problems go far beyond issues of faith.

Most Christian people have little suspicion and fear of contamination by medical doctors who are not believers. They accept as valid medical diagnoses and treatments offered by competent doctors whose religious beliefs are not compatible with their faith. I believe the time has come when we can begin to have the same attitude toward the treatment of emotional and mental problems. In many ways, the mental health disciplines have come of age. They are no longer deliberately and universally antagonistic toward Christianity, and, most important of all, are now well populated by Christians who are solid in their faith and who know how to mobilize the power of God and his Spirit to bring total healing.

## Professional Treatment of Depression

The specific treatment methods for depression fall into three general categories: psychotherapy, medication, and physical treatment. In practice these methods are often combined to treat a specific depression problem.

In the remainder of this chapter I will be looking in detail at these three methods of treatment—not to provide a guide for self-treatment, but to help dispel some of the mystery and fear that has surrounded professional treatment for depression, and to give depressed people and their families some basis for evaluating the treatment they are receiving. Before discussing the methods of treatment in detail, however, I want to examine some general questions that are frequently asked about professional treatment:

(1) *When should professional treatment be sought?* There is no simple answer to this question. People differ in their ability to tolerate and recover from depression and in the internal and external resources available to them. It has been my experience that most Christians do not seek professional help soon enough. They delay admitting they have a problem until it has reached chronic proportions. Because the problem is in the realm of the mind, much mystery about treatment prevails. A minister who would readily seek medical help for pain or a physical problem is often reticent to seek specialized help for a mental problem.

When a person is clearly losing his or her grip on life, experiencing painful emotions which may be incapacitating, becoming ineffective in work, and destructive in interpersonal relationships, the time for professional help has clearly arrived. Depression that is extremely deep, that has lasted more than a month, or that is experienced repeatedly should be treated by a professional. It is important to remember that the sooner treatment of a severe depression is begun, the shorter its duration will be.

(2) *What type of professional treatment should be sought?* This depends on the nature and severity of the problem. Mild depressions of the reactive sort can be handled by a competent counselor with at least a master's degree in counseling. Clinical social workers and experienced pastoral counselors also work effectively with this type of problem. The more serious depressions and those that appear to be repetitive should be treated by a clinical psychologist or a psychiatrist

who is experienced in working in a hospital setting and with severely disturbed patients. If psychiatric help is needed, a competent counselor or psychologist will make an appropriate referral, whereas an incompetent counselor will tend to cling to patients even when he or she cannot help them. When the depression is psychotic in nature I advocate psychiatric treatment right at the outset, since medication and perhaps other physical forms of treatment will be required.

(3) *Should a Christian go only to a Christian psychologist or psychiatrist?* Whenever possible, yes. Treatment by someone who understands and shares the Christian faith can make a big difference in the level of trust and rapport between patient and therapist. Unfortunately, not every "Christian" professional is necessarily competent or skilled to deal with your particular problem. Also, in many parts of the country (and in many parts of the world), Christian mental-health professionals are not readily available. It may be necessary, therefore, to see someone who is not a Christian believer. If the professional is obviously competent, then this should not be a hindrance. However, if he or she appears to be antagonistic toward Christianity, it is probably best to see someone else. The hassle of defending one's beliefs to a hostile therapist is not worth the trouble.

On the whole, I would say that, if I had to choose between an understanding, competent, nonbelieving professional and an incompetent "Christian" professional, I would choose the former. Simply being a Christian does not necessarily give a therapist extra insight into the nature of a problem such as depression.

(4) *Should a depressed person tell others that he is seeking treatment?* This depends on a number of factors: the type of depression (short and milder depressions are not worth talking about), whom you are thinking about telling (some people are more understanding than others), how long you've known them (the longer the better), and how accepting you are of yourself (some people can be more transparent than others without its being destructive). It will be necessary to weigh all these factors carefully before deciding whether to publicize the depression or the treatment. A minister, of course, will need to consider how willing his congregation is to accept human weaknesses on the part of their pastor, as well as how long he has served in his present position.

## What Is Psychotherapy?

Literally speaking, psychotherapy means "treatment of the mind." It is the nonphysical form of treatment for problems of an emotional or behavioral nature in which one person helps to remedy disturbed emotions or patterns of behavior and promotes positive personality growth and development. In many respects psychotherapy means an acceleration of the growth of a person, an improvement in the ability to give and receive love, a change in debilitating beliefs and attitudes, and a balancing of values.

Unfortunately, psychotherapy is generally thought of only as a special type of treatment that takes place in the office of a psychologist or psychiatrist. This erroneous idea leads to a "guild" definition which artificially restricts the practice of psychotherapy to a limited number of disciplines. But while the law does specify that only persons with a certain educational and professional background may call themselves "psychotherapists," this does not mean that psychotherapy can only take place in the office of one of these professionals.

Actually, psychology in its most general sense is simply a way of thinking about, delving into, and solving problems of human existence. Professionals do not have a monopoly on it; in fact, the Holy Spirit is the most effective psychotherapist of all. The Christian church, through its ministry of preaching and fellowship, has been practicing psychotherapy for twenty centuries, and whenever a pastor counsels, he is doing psychotherapy. Practically every human relationship has psychotherapeutic implications. Marriage is an ongoing relationship of psychotherapy, just as parent/child relationships and general friendships are. There is really nothing mystical about psychotherapy; it is primarily a process of one person's showing love and understanding to someone else.

But while psychotherapy in a broad sense is part of every human interaction, in its more specific sense it does refer to the work of a professional—someone who is specially trained and employed in using a knowledge of human interaction to help people solve emotional or other problems. It is not the province of any one discipline, however. Clinical psychologists, psychiatrists, clinical social workers, psychiatric nurses, marriage and family counselors, and pastoral counselors are all trained in aspects of psychotherapy; the essential differences are in the range of problems in which expertise in treatment can be claimed.

## Why Are Professional Psychotherapists Needed?

There are important differences between the love and advice of a caring friend, spouse, or even minister and the skill of a professional psychotherapist. Besides the special knowledge and understanding of the human mind the professional has acquired, the most important difference is that friends will tend to be subjective and too sympathetic.

They will have difficulty not imposing their own views, values, and convictions on the person who needs help. Good professional psychotherapists, on the other hand, are trained to be objective, to know when their urges or interests are intruding, and to be unaffected by any new behaviors or emotions the person in therapy might wish to experiment with. Their role is to be closer than any friend, yet distant enough that they can walk away from the relationship without causing this leaving to be perceived as a loss.

Since the process of professional psychotherapy is now well understood and based on scientific rather than philosophical premises, its practice should be quite acceptable to Christians. The human mind is extremely complex, and the specialized research and study of how it works can help people heal and change. (Of course, as in the case of general medicine, much of what happens merely aids the processes God has already created.) The professional psychotherapist, therefore, can offer an effective and efficient way of healing through his specialized skills. If these skills are integrated with an understanding of God's will, purpose, and saving power, they can enhance the work of the Holy Spirit and not usurp it.

As a Christian psychotherapist, I find that Christ is central in all my work. Although much improvement in personal functioning can take place without reference to spiritual issues (for example, a snake phobia can be treated without mentioning Christian values), I always feel that the practice of psychotherapy from a purely "secular" base leaves much to be desired. It only provides a beginning; the real joys of living are found in Christ, not just in personality growth or improvement in emotional functioning. I believe the best psychotherapy always has as its ultimate goal the realization of all that God intends for his heirs—spiritual as well as psychological.

## What Types of Psychotherapy Are Used for Depression?

The major types of psychotherapy can be categorized by their primary points of emphasis. They can be divided into two major groups: nonreconstructive and reconstructive.

The nonreconstructive therapies are primarily "supportive"; their goal is the alleviation of symptoms. Nonreconstructive psychotherapies include many "counseling" systems such as family counseling; desensitizations; vocational counseling; occupational therapies; support groups; dance, music, and art therapies; and pastoral counseling.

Reconstructive therapies go beyond this and attempt to bring about changes in basic personality structure. These tend to be long-term therapies, whereas the nonreconstructive kind are short-term. Since reconstructive psychotherapies are generally more important in the treatment of depression, I will provide a description of the most common approaches:

(1) *Psychoanalysis.* Ranging from pure psychoanalysis to Jungian and ego psychology, this approach focuses more on issues such as the effects of early development and the control of unconscious factors. Treatment tends to take longer than other approaches and is confined mainly to treating character and severe neurotic disorders.

(2) *Client-centered therapy.* This approach, developed by Dr. Carl Rogers, is designed to facilitate the expression and clarification of feelings and to build self-esteem. Every therapist should have embodied into his or her therapeutic style the three qualities which Dr. Rogers claims are essential to the healing relationship: unconditional positive regard for the client, congruence (the therapist acting honestly with the client), and empathic understanding (the therapist accurately sensing the feeling state of the client). These qualities are very similar to the "love" which Christians are encouraged by the New Testament to have toward each other.

(3) *Behavior modification therapy.* Following mainly the techniques of operant conditioning presented by Dr. B. F. Skinner, behavior modification avoids exploring the past and concentrates on using certain learning principles to teach new behaviors. It is not intended to be a treatment for every problem, but is very effective in habit disorders, phobias, and in correcting personality weaknesses such as underassertiveness. Behavioral techniques are used by many therapists for dealing with specific problems.

(4) *Cognitive therapies.* This approach basically uses reasoning to modify beliefs and attitudes, and to improve logic. Victor Frankl's "logotherapy" and Glasser's "reality therapy" can be considered to be forms of cognitive therapy. One current popular form is known as "rational emotive therapy," which has been developed by Dr. Albert Ellis.

(5) *Transactional analysis.* Developed by Dr. Eric Berne, it is basically a popularized version of ego psychology and focuses on the interactions or "transactions" between people. The concepts are easily understood by lay persons and can powerfully modify behavior by providing an easy "handle" on what is happening in relationships.

(6) *Gestalt therapy.* A variation of psychoanalysis which attempts to help the person who is in therapy to achieve a stable internal structure. It encourages awareness and the experiencing of feelings. Gestalt techniques are often used by therapists of many schools.

(7) *Existential analysis.* Coming from a philosophical concern over

the essence of existence and the meaning of life, this approach is becoming increasingly popular. It is more a way of thinking than a set of techniques, and has been adopted by therapists of many persuasions. In many ways, while there is no "Christian psychotherapy" as such, the concerns of this "school" are very much compatible with those of most Christian psychotherapists.

Other minor "schools" of reconstructive psychotherapy are mostly offshoots of those mentioned above. Most therapists tend to be "eclectic"; that is, they draw on the specific techniques of many of these kinds of therapy, tailoring them to specific problems. There is no generally accepted "Christian psychotherapy," although many Christian psychotherapists have integrated faith issues with therapeutic techniques.

## How Does One Choose a Psychotherapist?

There are a number of factors to be considered when choosing a psychotherapist for the treatment of depression:
—Has the therapist the necessary training to be able to differentiate psychological from endogenous depressions? This is a crucial question, since much time and money can be wasted treating endogenous depression only with psychological techniques.
—Is he or she open to the use of antidepressant medication if it is necessary?
—If not a Christian, is he or she understanding of and sympathetic to Christian beliefs?
—What is his or her particular theoretical orientation? Is the depressed person comfortable with this orientation, or will it be antagonistic to his or her faith?

To locate a psychotherapist, ministers or Christian workers can begin by consulting their personal physicians or by talking with other Christian workers in their locality. Another good source of information about Christian therapists would be one of the Christian schools of psychology such as Fuller Theological Seminary Graduate School of Psychology (177 North Madison Avenue, Pasadena, CA 91101) or Rosemead Graduate School of Professional Psychology (Biola University, 13800 Biola Avenue, La Mirada, CA 90638). These schools keep a national register of practicing Christian psychologists. Two national Christian organizations that publish membership directories of mental-health professionals in various fields are The Christian Association for Psychological Studies (University Hills Christian Center, 27000 Farmington Road, Farmington Hills, MI 48018) and the Christian Medical Society (1122 Westgate, Oak Park, IL 60301).

Regardless of references, however, if a depressed person does not feel comfortable with a therapist after three or four sessions, then he or she should feel free to change to someone else. The nature of psychotherapy is such that the client must feel comfortable and be confident that the therapist knows what he or she is doing.

One final word about psychotherapy: It can be expensive. But most major medical insurance provides coverage for psychotherapy when it is provided by a psychiatrist or psychologist. (If a person covered by medical insurance requires hospitalization for depression, the chances are very high that he or she could be reimbursed for half to 80 percent of the cost.) In addition, there are public and private agencies that provide certain kinds of psychotherapy for fees charged on a sliding scale according to income. (Many cities have information and referral services that can provide information about such agencies—check the yellow pages.) Some private therapists will provide ministers with special rates and will even allow patients to make time payments for their treatment. With the many and varied resources now available, there is no reason why a person needing the help psychotherapy can offer should have to do without treatment for financial reasons.

## Antidepressant Medication

Antidepressant drugs are of relatively recent origin; they were introduced about 1955. Since then, however, they have revolutionized the treatment of severe depressions. Prior to their availability, the use of insulin shock and electroconvulsive therapy was widespread. While these forms of treatment were effective, they were also inconvenient and cumbersome. Antidepressant medication provided a simple, effective, and nondisruptive method of treatment and is now the most widely used method of treating those depressions which are suspected of having biological causes.

As in the case of psychotherapy, however, much misunderstanding and misinformation about antidepressant medication persists, and this caused unnecessary resistance to its use in treating depression. In part, this is due to a concern about the abuse of drugs in general. Over the past ten years we have become increasingly aware that the cure can sometimes be worse than the disease. We have heard of cases in which the overprescribing of tranquilizers (Valium, Librium) or stimulants (diet pills) has led to addiction and other problems. In addition, many Christians are suspicious of the use of drugs because they fear it leads to taking the easy way out—relying on artificial means to solve the problems of living.

On the whole, these concerns are justified, but in the case of anti-depressant medication they are generally unfounded. There are two important reasons:

(1) *The antidepressant drugs are only effective in the treatment of the endogenous and psychotic forms of depression.* In other words, they generally do *not* help those depressions which are the result of life problems—the reactive or neurotic depressions. They do not, therefore, take away an individual's responsibility to put his or her life in order. (In cases where antidepressants *do* appear to help those suffering from reactive depressions, the alleviation of symptoms can usually be attributed to a placebo effect or a mild sedation some kinds of anti-depressants may cause.)

(2) *The antidepressants are not habit-forming or addictive.* Unlike tranquilizers and stimulants, antidepressants do not produce any immediate improvement in mood. They require a two- to three-week build-up in the body before they become therapeutic. Because the patient receives no instant alleviation of symptoms, there is no urge to take the medication. If anything, the opposite is usually the problem. The effects are so delayed that the user easily loses interest and must be constantly urged to keep up the medication level in the body. This is a situation which definitely does not favor drug dependency.

It may be helpful at this point to explain just what antidepressant drugs are and how they work. Most importantly, they are *not* stimulants; in fact, antidepressants are sometimes called "psychic energizers" to differentiate them from the stimulant drugs. Stimulants such as the amphetamines sometimes used in diet pills and the caffeine found in colas and coffee act to artificially "rev up" the nervous system. While stimulants may sometimes be used to treat low-grade depression, they are usually not a good idea because the "up" they provide only lasts for a short time. In addition, they cause the body to use up its reserves and thus create the potential for nervous collapse and mental exhaustion. They also can lead to physical or psychological addiction. They should not be used at all unless one's physician insists—and gives good reasons for prescribing them.

The nonstimulant antidepressants, on the other hand, do *not* activate the nervous system. They work by helping restore a chemical imbalance at the junctions ("synapses") between nerve cells and thus ensure proper functioning of the nervous system. The action is restorative rather than stimulative.

## When Are Antidepressants Used?

Antidepressant medication is used to treat those depressions which are suspected of having biological causes, including the endogenous forms. Occasionally they are given for depressions that may be the result of external factors to reduce the effect of underlying endogenous components.

However, let me hasten to add that, while this type of medication works best on endogenous depression, it is not always easy to know whether or not a given depression is endogenous. One endogenous form, for instance, reveals itself merely as an exaggerated tendency toward reactive depression. I believe that *many* such depressions are not properly treated because psychotherapists, believing that there is an adequate environmental explanation for the depression, fail to recognize this endogenous predisposition.

A valuable indicator of the presence of endogenous depression and the potential efficacy of antidepressant medication has recently been developed. Known as the Dexamethasone Suppression Test (or DST), it can provide rapid confirmation that antidepressant medication will be effective in a given case of depression. The test serves as a "marker" identifying that subgroup of depression most likely to be endogenous.

While the test is still undergoing some refinement, it is now widely used and readily available. The procedure is simple: A small dose of a drug called dexamethasone is taken the night before the test, and two blood samples are taken at 8:00 A.M. and 4:00 P.M. The results are available in a day or two without great inconvenience and with no risk or discomfort.

The alternative to the DST is the trial use of an antidepressant for three to four weeks. If the depression lifts, it was probably endogenous. If it doesn't improve, some other form of treatment is called for. But clearly this simple new test, which is quicker, more accurate, and eliminates the possiblity of unnecessary side effects, is a better choice in most cases where an endogenous depression is suspected.

## What Are the Disadvantages of Antidepressants?

For the average person, there are hardly any disadvantages to short-term use of antidepressant medication. In cases where antidepressants are prescribed for extended periods of time, regular physical examinations can help ensure that the patient does not experience any harmful side effects. Three potential problems must be considered when the antidepressants are prescribed:

(1) *The impact of side effects.* While some minor side effects are

experienced by most users, they typically only last a few days. Dry mouth, slight dizziness, and minor stomach problems are the most common complaints, and can usually be ignored. However, if these problems persist more than eight or ten days, the physician should be consulted; he will probably want to prescribe another drug. Alcohol and certain other drugs should not be taken with antidepressants. The prescribing physician should provide warnings about these.

(2) *The presence of physical problems.* The physical conditions that can contraindicate antidepressants are high blood pressure and eye problems such as glaucoma. Frequent medical examinations may be necessary for patients with these problems who take antidepressant medication. Again, the physician will know what to look for. Antidepressant medication should *never* be taken without medical monitoring.

(3) *The likelihood of a special sensitivity to one particular drug.* Some antidepressant medications may create a problem for a given person who may have a special sensitivity. Unusual or exaggerated side-effects will be an indication of this.

On the whole, problems in medication are relatively rare and nothing we have discussed should be cause for alarm. These drugs are almost always safe to use.

## Which Is the Best Antidepressant Drug?

There is no "best" drug for treating depression. The medication must be tailored to the form of depression and the characteristics of the depressed person. People differ greatly in their responses to medication. Sometimes a combination of drugs is most effective, so more than one may be prescribed.

Antidepressant drugs in the treatment of depression fall into three categories:

(1) *MAO (mono-amine oxidase) inhibitors.* The MAO inhibitors act to restrict the ability of a certain enzyme to break down serotonin, an important brain chemical. The inhibitory effect of the MAO therefore raises the level of serotonin and other brain chemicals, and this in turn alleviates the depression. The three most often used MAO inhibitors are Marplan, Nardil, and Parnate. While MAO inhibitors are effective in treating atypical depressions, the side effects are more noticeable and treatment may need to be undertaken in a hospital setting. These drugs are therefore used mainly as a last resort, and only if tricyclics are not effective.

(2) *Tricyclic derivatives.* The tricyclics are the most important group of antidepressant drugs currently available. Their mode of action is to

increase the level of serotonin and other brain chemicals by direct stimulation. The overall effect is a reduction in the depression symptomology.

The more common tricyclics are shown below:

| *Generic Name* | *Brand Name* |
|---|---|
| Imipramine | Tofranil |
| Amitriptyline | Elavil |
| Nortriptyline | Aventyl |
| Doxepin | Sinequan |
| Doxepin | Adapin |
| Desipramine | Norpramin |
| Desipramine | Pertofrane |
| Protriptyline | Vivactil |
| Perphenazine and Amitriptyline | Triavil |

(3) *Lithium Carbonate*. For the specific treatment of a special form of depression, manic-depressive psychosis, lithium carbonate (Lithane) is often the drug of choice. This medication has the opposite effect of the MAO inhibitors. It corrects the overactivity of the catecholamines seen in the "manic" phase of this particular disorder and is also used to treat the "depressive" phase. Lithium can prevent relapses in patients with recurrent mood disorders and is currently being found helpful in treating the premenstrual syndrome (often characterized by a deep depression), emotionally unstable character disorders, and general hyperactivity. Recently, the widespread use of lithium in general depression has become quite common.

It is important to remember that none of these drugs acts like antibiotics to "cure" the disorder. They restore and maintain normal nervous system functioning while the natural healing process takes place. Perhaps one day we will have a curative medication but, for now, support for weak nervous systems is all we can expect.

## How Long Is Drug Treatment Carried On?

The effectiveness of drug treatment depends to a great extent on the skill of the prescribing physician. The "tailoring" of the right drug or combination of drugs takes careful evaluation of many factors, including the patient's personality structure, background, and physical condition. Underdosage in the early stage of treatment is very common and can be as bad as no treatment at all. Just how high a dosage can be tolerated will depend on the patient, the patient's attitude toward drugs, and the extent to which the medication disrupts the patient's work and daily functioning.

The tricyclics may take as long as four or even five weeks to show any benefit. If after that period of time they are not effective, they should be phased out slowly. A physician will know the appropriate timetable.

One very important recent research finding is that the chances of recovery increase and greater improvement can be expected when drug treatment is combined with other procedures such as psychotherapy, even when the depression is clearly endogenous. Presumably, this is because there are many secondary factors of a psychological nature that serve to prolong or intensify a depression.

## Physical Methods of Treatment

The two most important physical forms of treatment for depression are hospitalization and electroconvulsive therapy (ECT):

(1) *Hospitalization.* A brief stay in a hospital environment can be very effective in stopping a "runaway" or spiraling depression. Being removed from the pressures of work and routine duties can relieve the apprehension and anxiety accompanying severe depression and establish a more solid foundation for continued treatment.

Hospitalization allows a more efficient establishment of correct dosages of medication. Also, intensive psychotherapy, usually on a daily basis, can be provided in a supportive environment. Consequently, more rapid recovery can often be expected, especially in the acute forms of depression.

(2) *Electroconvulsive therapy.* First used in Italy during the late 1930s, ECT became widespread as a treatment procedure after the Second World War. While the advent of antidepressant medication has reduced the need for ECT, it is still the most effective and efficient treatment for moderate to severe depressions. Despite misinformation given to the public through the melodrama of books, TV, and the movies, ECT remains a reliable, effective, and quick way of treating severe depression. (Medication may be less frightening, but it takes longer.) While ECT cannot be administered without the concurrence of at least two psychiatrists, the treatment is relatively harmless when administered by a competent psychiatrist.

ECT is administered under a general anesthetic. A muscle relaxant is used to avoid injury. A mild current is then applied to the temples and a brief seizure occurs. The whole procedure is over in a matter of minutes. It may take a total of only eight to ten treatments at the rate of two to three a week for an endogenous depression to show improvement, and up to twelve or fourteen for a more severe depression—this is considerably quicker than medication.

Often the treatment is administered to just one side of the brain to minimize the side effects. A careful physical examination always precedes treatment. The only unpleasant side effects may be an occasional headache, nausea, and perhaps a mild memory loss for recent events. These usually occur only for a short period of time after each treatment.

Unfortunately, not everyone is a candidate for ECT. Cardiovascular disorders, infections, or advanced age would make ECT an unwise choice of treatment for an individual. Otherwise, the procedure is painless, less bothersome than taking medication over many months, and—with modern day precautions—extremely safe.

# 11

## WHY MINISTERS BURN OUT

"Burnout" is a phenomenon that is increasingly becoming a serious problem among doctors, nurses, counselors, social workers, and others in the helping professions. And ministers, devout and dedicated though they may be, are not free of it.

Defining and describing burnout is difficult because it takes different forms for different people. One person may constantly complain about being overworked and underpaid or continously grumble about his co-workers. Another may feel that God has shut the heavens and no longer has any interest in him. Still another may sit at her desk staring at papers for long hours, making little effort to answer letters or to complete reports awaiting attention. A person experiencing burnout may drive around aimlessly for hours or park in a lonely spot to sit and brood. A faithful and loving husband may allow himself to have an affair with a naïve, hysterical counselee. Or another may secretly turn to alcohol.

Whatever its specific form, burnout generally leads to a progressive loss of ambition, idealism, energy, calling, and purpose. For the minister, untreated burnout can often mean the beginning of the end of a career.

Burnout can be seen as a direct result of certain conditions inherent in the work of those in the helping or "human services" professions. (It doesn't occur nearly so often in business circles.) Among the conditions which contribute to the incidence of burnout are: insufficient training for complex work with other humans, work overload with no clear work boundaries, too many hours spent doing work that is not appreciated, too much "politics" and too little Christian charity, too much bureaucratic constraint with too little work flexibility, too great a gap between aspiration and accomplishment. Ministry has a high potential for all of these adverse conditions.

## The Relationship of Burnout to Depression

Burnout produces depression in two ways:

(1) *The physiological protective systems of the individual begin to break down under the prolonged stresses of unsatisfactory working conditions (a state of distress).* The human body was not designed to sustain long periods of stress. Under continual pressure, protective and regulatory mechanisms become disturbed and the emergency system of the body uses up its reserves. Consequently, the person becomes less flexible, more guarded and sensitive, and depression ensues. In such cases the depression is both a protective mechanism and a reaction to the increased possibility of loss that comes from a diminished physical capacity for coping with life and work.

(2) *Much of what is happening is experienced by the individual as loss or deprivation.* The further along the burnout path a person goes, the more potential for loss there is. Perception becomes warped, so that even normal and happy events come to seem negative. Rational thinking becomes more and more difficult. In other words, under continual stress, healthy psychological mechanisms gradually become distorted.

The depression that accompanies burnout is characterized by apathy—a progressive emotional detachment from life in the face of increasing frustration. Workers who started their careers caring about others end up being preoccupied with themselves, and this shift of focus is accompanied by an attitude of resignation.

## The Christian Worker's Trap

In the face of burnout, many people-helpers are able to retreat from commitment without much guilt. They learn to go through the motions of work with the attitude, "I do my job as best I can, but I just can't let myself care too much whether people are helped." But most ministers and other Christian workers find it difficult, if not impossible, to adopt this detached attitude. The high degree of internal control, the belief that the work is a high and special calling, and the need to approach God regularly force such people to resist retreat. Sometimes this only intensifies their depression because they feel trapped.

There are, of course, many ministers who never experience burnout, and I don't want to give the impression that the ministry or Christian work is always bound to be devastating to those who are called into it.

As I have mentioned earlier, there are many compensations, not the least of which is the joy of Christian service and time spent performing duties for which God provides his own special blessing. However, I think it is important for Christians to be aware that the vocation is fraught with pitfalls that can provide all the conditions for burnout. The wise pastor or Christian worker will be aware of these conditions, be on the lookout for its telltale signs, and thus be better prepared to energize the coping skills needed to avoid the burnout trap.

## How the Nature of the Work Makes Ministers Loss-Prone

The nature of ministry provides a number of situations conducive to the experience of loss and therefore to burnout and depression. Some of these were alluded to in chapter 2, where we discussed the emotional hazards of the ministry. Here the discussion will focus specifically on the concept of loss as it relates to depression in the ministry. My goal in this chapter will be to provide the reader with a better understanding of these losses, thus improving his or her ability to anticipate and recognize loss-provoking situations.

(1) *Ministry is people oriented.* As a built-in source of frustration, other people are a major cause of burnout, and yet *people* is what ministry is all about! Whenever people work with people, there are bound to be intense interactions, misunderstandings, miscommunications, ulterior motives, and the like. But nowhere in the human services is this more likely to occur and be as damaging as in the ministry. The reasons are twofold.

First, when ministers begin their careers they are often *not as well trained* in handling conflict situations, difficult personalities, and communication problems as are social workers, psychologists, counselors, and teachers. Training for these latter professions places a high priority on human relationships, and skills in these areas are deliberately developed. This is usually not the case in seminaries, which tend to place more emphasis on theological study and preaching. By the time a young minister realizes he or she has problems relating to people, poor habits of communication and people management may have become established and difficult to break. (One way to alter this problem, of course, would be to place greater emphasis on relationship skills in the training of ministers. It is also important for ministers to continue working on these skills after seminary.)

Second, ministers relate mostly to people in a *voluntary structure.* Church congregations are made up of people who *choose* to be there, and who can just as easily choose *not* to be! Many church members participate when they feel things are going well but disappear when problems develop. Now, it is human nature to want to be on a winning team, but it is the nature of church life and Christian endeavor that one does not always know when one is winning. Sowing must come before reaping, and sowing again must follow the reaping. Most church members love to "reap" but find the "sowing" tedious and unexciting; as a result, many of them will simply not be around when it's time for the hard, seemingly unrewarding work to be done.

(Of course, there are also many dedicated and consistent church members who have their priorities straight and who can be counted on to be at their posts no matter what. But a minister is blessed if more than 20 percent of his congregation are in this category. There are still many others who can be sources of frustration, conflict, and bitter disagreement.)

Another reason the voluntary structure of church work can lead to problems for ministers is that the people they must work with in the church are not necessarily the ones they would have chosen if they were actually hiring co-workers. As leaders of a mostly volunteer organization, they must relate to many with whom they would not normally have any affinity. This can lead to growth, but it can also cause personality conflicts.

The voluntary nature of church life puts the minister under strain. This is inevitable and must be accepted; a minister has to build immunity to it. Putting together committees, motivating workers, resolving conflicts, mobilizing resources, and carrying out the many other tasks which characterize ministry can cause a minister to feel as if he or she were running a race on a greased surface or trying to plug a twelve-inch hole in a dyke with one finger! But this is simply the nature of work with volunteer organizations.

A church can't be run like an army (where one person gives orders and everyone else obeys) nor like a business (where the boss pays employees to do his bidding). In many respects, this is just as well. God's church is a unique institution in which everyone has equal status and value. It is likened in Scripture to a body with many parts—all necessary and equal in importance. Getting the parts of this body to work well together is challenging and immensely satisfying work, but it is also extremely difficult. Perhaps our biggest errors occur when we usurp the work of the Holy Spirit as the harmonizer, healer, and helper in this task. The enormity and complexity of organizing a volunteer institution should make us depend more than ever on divine resources.

I have found that many ministers work against themselves by placing too much emphasis on the achievement of goals and undervaluing the process by which those goals are reached. This has been especially true in recent years, when some ministers have been strongly influenced by high pressure business notions such as management by objective, critical path scheduling, and so on. Techniques like these need to be used with caution in organizations such as churches where volunteers make up a large percentage of the work force. While they may improve some aspects of church functioning—most specifically staff management—and while some unique church settings may respond well to strongly goal-oriented approaches, a volunteer organization is not always predictable or successful when put under this sort of pressure. People tend to retreat or rebel when "managed" too strongly.

Now, it's important not to misunderstand what I am saying. I am not saying goals should be eliminated; goals are important because they tell us where we are going. But there needs to be a *balance* in emphasis between the goals themselves and the process by which those goals are reached. In a church setting the process is at least as important as the goals themselves. In fact, I believe it is ultimately that process—not the achievement of arbitrarily set goals—which actually builds God's kingdom.

Let me explain further. Suppose the Sunday school committee, under the direction of their pastor, set as their goal for the coming year an increase of 50 percent in student enrollment. Everyone agrees that this is reasonable and desirable. But suppose that at the end of the year, with all the best efforts that could be mustered, the enrollment is found to have increased only 25 percent. Will the minister and the committee feel they have failed? If their focus is only on achieving goals, they will. But if they value the things that have been achieved and discovered in the process of working toward the goals, they may have a different perspective. They may be able to see that in the process of working toward their goal new friendships have been formed, new commitments made, new skills developed, and a new spirit discovered. People may have learned to love more, to be less defensive and more forgiving. Their goal of a 50 percent increase gave them direction, but even though that goal was not achieved the process of working toward it may have been profoundly effective. Surely it was in that process that the real work of God was being done.

In my experience, whenever I have encountered too much preoccupation with goal achievement on the part of a minister, I have invariably found that pastor had a strong tendency toward depression. I have come to believe that strongly goal-oriented ministers will almost inevitably experience more frustration than process-oriented ones. Blind spots are easily enlarged by this preoccupation, which I like to call "goal myopia."

(2) *There are no clear boundaries in the minister's work.* As a psychologist, I usually know when my workday is over. When my last

patient leaves, I gather my papers together, pick up my briefcase, and head home. I may have some notes I want to go over or a book I would like to review, but I am still able to feel I've successfully finished my day's work.

But when is a minister ever done for the day? The task of pastoring is a formidable one. No pastor can ever visit enough, pray enough, study enough, prepare sermons enough, or be involved enough in social issues. He may not be in an office eight hours a day, but he is always "on call"—and he never has weekends off! It is easy, therefore, for the minister to continually feel that his work is never finished, that he can barely cope with the immediate demands on his time, let alone catch up on the backlog. It is hard for him to feel a sense of "closure" or completeness when he finally heads home for an evening.

But such a sense of being "through for the day" is very important both psychologically and physiologically. One of the major causes of stress disorders—including depression—is a chronic feeling of incompleteness and a pervasive anxiety about tasks still needing attention. This keeps the various systems in the body from switching off and returning to a relaxed, restful state.

Part of my work as a clinical psychologist is taken up with teaching patients how to cope with stress. Using electronic instruments that measure heart rate, muscle tension, skin temperature, brain electrical waves, and skin resistance, I often demonstrate to patients how responsive their bodies are to the stimulation of their environment and how it remains alerted for action even though the stimulation is removed. If their mental attitude is "I can't let down now; there's too much to do," or "I've not completed a fraction of what I wanted to do," their various physiological systems will be kept in a state of alertness and activity. Such is the state of people who never feel that their day's chores are done. In due course this state becomes chronic and produces many of the stress-related and psychosomatic disorders that are so prevalent today.

To avoid the stress that results from such a continual state of alertness, a clear message must be sent to the body at the end of every day that it can relax and begin the process of rest and recovery. But how do pastors do this? How do they ascertain that a reasonable day's work has been done?

Since the work of pastoring contains no clear inherent boundaries, it is usually necessary to *create* boundaries and to courageously apply them. This is perhaps most effectively accomplished by preparing lists of daily goals and "checking off" the tasks as they are accomplished. But it is extremely important to be realistic about making up these lists, writing down only what can actually be accomplished and allowing plenty of time for interruptions, emergencies, and unexpected chores. The notion that a person can "stretch" himself or herself into doing more work by making the "to do" list longer is simply incorrect. It is more likely that a too-long list will increase the possibility of depression by emphasizing the feeling of never completing a day's work.

If there are undone tasks at the end of the day for two or three days in a row, the list needs to be shortened until it can successfully be followed. There's nothing like success to breed motivation and nothing like coping to engender feelings of being successful. The genuine feeling of accomplishment that comes from successfully completing a list of realistic work goals can go a long way toward preventing depression in a minister or Christian worker.

(3) *A minister often lacks criteria for measuring work accomplishment.* When does a pastor feel successful? When large numbers of people come to church? When the church budget reaches a certain enormous figure? When a predetermined number of new members join in a given period of time? When an extra worship service must be added? Every experienced pastor knows how elusive and misleading such criteria can be.

Many pastors play games with themselves at this point. They downplay their concern with numbers and statistics and keep telling themselves such tangible "proofs of success" are not important. Unfortunately they often *are* important—not necessarily for God's kingdom, but for the minister's self-esteem! For at the root of the "numbers" dilemma is the fact that ministry presents problems in defining what is successful pastoring.

People coming into the ministry from other areas of endeavor often say that it is far more difficult to set standards for evaluating their accomplishments in the ministry than it was in their previous employment. I understand this problem because I experienced a similar one when I moved from engineering into psychology many years ago. My engineering accomplishments still stand—bridges, reservoirs, buildings, and freeways. They are easily recognizable, enduring, and satisfying. But where are my psychological accomplishments? Sure, there are many—healed hearts, homes and bodies. But they are not as tangible and easy to pinpoint as those of engineering. And pastors may find it even harder to identify their accomplishments once they get their eyes off money, buildings, and church attendance. This can lead to feelings of loss and the creation of chronic depression.

What is the solution? It is not an easy one, I'm sorry to say. We are so oriented to our senses that we cannot believe what we don't actually see. If we cannot measure and evaluate our progress we find it hard to accept that any has taken place. The only way to overcome this limitation is to tune into God's standards and constantly hone our values and beliefs so as to be in touch with God's eternal criteria of success—faithfulness. Any pastor who takes his eyes off the values God holds highest is bound to be prone to depression. We must train ourselves to distrust overt symbols of success. We are called to be obedient, not successful; the ambition of obedience is qualitatively different from that of success. Therefore we need to be wary lest the warning apply to us:

> I will spue thee out of my mouth, because thou sayest, "I am successful and rich with large church buildings, and increased with large attendances and have need of no humility"; and knowest not that thou are wretched, and miserable, and poor, and blind, and naked [with apologies to the writer of Rev. 3:16–17, but I think this is a legitimate application of the verse's true meaning].

(4) *The minister is often put on a pedestal.* Ministers occupy a position of high visibility, and their calling carries with it a great amount of honor and distinction. Although over the past fifty years significant changes have come about that have diminished the prestige somewhat, ministers still tend to be put on a pedestal by those around them. Who in a church is more sought after as friend and confidant than the pastor? Whose opinion is more respected? Whatever he or she says will be listened to and people will think and talk about his or her ideas. Members will invite others to their church saying, "Come and hear our minister; he [she] preaches so beautifully," or "You must come and see what our youth pastor does for young people."

Such prominence and high visibility creates certain hazards for the minister. One is pride; someone has said that "few are tempted to become so vain so often as the preacher." But even more difficult for most ministers is the problem of living up to expectations. Ministers may be respected and admired in their churches, but they are also expected by their parishioners to behave, talk, and believe in a certain way. Often they are expected to be better than everyone else, more resistant to temptation and above reproach. Such expectations may even be self-generated; for example, a pastor might say to himself or herself, "Well, since I am the pastor, I had better not do this or that."

The trouble with these internal and external expectations is that they are often unrealistic and cannot be met. A pastor, being human, is bound to fail occasionally and not live up to expectations. And because of the high visibility, people *know* when he or she fails. Many kinds of losses may result from this situation—loss of self-respect and the respect of others, threatened loss of prestige and power, and so on.

Depression in the minister can be a direct result of failing to live up to the expectations the pedestal position creates.

Depression can also be a result of the constant struggle to maintain and maximize the popularity that being on a pedestal brings to a minister. It is a rare person who is devoid of any desire to be popular; we all like to be liked and we like the power popularity brings us. But no one—not even a minister on a pedestal—can be popular with everybody, or popular all the time. Difficulties can arise when ministers come to depend too much on their own popularity and try too hard to keep it at any cost.

Such ministers will lean one way and make public utterances to appease one group, only to find that another group takes umbrage. They may decide to remain silent on certain issues and to walk a middle path in their preaching, but still find there are eager hands waiting to drag them off their tightrope. They may even decide, "I'm going to preach solely for the approval of God and not of man," and then, after a period of total alienation from their congregations, realize they have actually been preaching out of anger and resentment toward the people who disagree with them—not out of God's leading. The pedestal of popularity is fraught with loss potential for the minister who values it too highly. But knowing the problems that can occur can help ministers avoid them entirely or at least not overreact when they do happen as a natural consequence of the nature of the work.

One final reason being on a pedestal position can be a problem is that the minister's family is usually put on a pedestal too! He or she is not the only one being watched closely; his or her spouse and children are also on display. And since they don't necessarily feel the need to comply with the many expectations the congregation and the minister may place on them, there is a high potential for conflict and resentment over this issue.

To minimize such difficulties, it is crucial that ministers learn very early in their careers that they can't please everybody—and neither can their families. They must give their spouse and children permission to be themselves; imposing their own or the congregation's expectations on the family will only breed resentment. Of course, it is important for ministers to clarify their expectations for their families by testing their expectations against the reality of God's Word and his plan for their lives, then to set their course clearly and unequivocally. But this must be done in close communication with the family, with careful listening and respect for what they have to say.

One final word on this issue of a minister's high visibility and need to live up to expectations: A few years ago I wanted to learn to sail. It didn't seem like a difficult skill to master so I bought a boat and I decided I would teach myself (with the aid of a good "how to" book). My strategy was this: When I was out at sea I would stay close to another boat and see how its skipper had set his sails, then I would do the same for mine. But it never worked; I would lose speed and sometimes go "into irons" (pointing dead into the wind in a state of complete helplessness). What was my mistake? The same one that so many ministers make. They think they can set the sail of their preaching style, or their philosophy of ministry, or their family, by doing what others do—by being a copy of someone else.

Boats are like ministers—or the other way around! Each is unique. Each requires a personalized course of direction, and the course sailed must be true and consistent, no matter how the winds of popularity may change or in which direction those around are sailing. When ministers do this with their lives, they keep to a minimum the experience of loss resulting from the nature of their work.

## Loss Proneness May Result from the Person of the Minister

The most important thing ministers bring to their ministry is themselves. True, they have spiritual resources and can draw on the power of the Holy Spirit; without that asset it would be better not to embark on the career of ministry at all. But it is still the *person* of the minister who is the channel of those spiritual resources. What are some of the qualities a minister brings to his work that are likely to be sources of loss and hence depression?

(1) *Certain personality traits may contribute to situations of loss.* This first and most obvious factor in a minister's work can be a major cause of loss experiences. All of us have certain aspects of our personalities that are negative as well as other aspects that are positive. And certain personality characteristics by their very nature can cause repeated problems either by creating clashes with others or by entrapping the person who displays those traits in unpleasant situations. Obvious examples of such negative personality characteristics are excessive anger, underdeveloped guilt responses, or antisocial tendencies; these are so blatantly destructive that they don't require exposition. But there are other, less obvious traits that may also cause serious problems.

Take, for example, the perfectionistic personality. This is not just the person who is overconscientious about doing things well; rather, it is the person who is obsessive and compulsive about it. There is a vast difference between wanting to do things well and being perfectionistic; one important difference is that the perfectionist has a built-in system of punishment for failing to reach perfection. The self-punishment is usually an inner-directed rage which robs the self of esteem and sets up a state of depression. Some psychologists speak of it as "anger turned inwards." Whatever it is, it is very self-destructive. At heart perfectionists are overcompensating for feelings of inferiority. They doubt their basic self-worth and are therefore constantly trying to prove to themselves that they are worthy. Their desks are kept impeccably clean. Every letter must be perfectly written and typed. They feel an obsessive need to do everything extremely well. Efficiency and effectiveness are not the real objectives; they do what they do because it is the only way they can feel comfortable.

Such a personality trait is bound to cause problems since the task of ministry is so comprehensive and limitless that no one can feel perfect in every aspect of its accomplishment. Loss will persistently stare into the face of a perfectionistic minister. Correcting perfectionistic tendencies may sometimes require extended psychotherapy, although working to deliberately ignore perfectionistic urges may be helpful.

The authoritarian type of personality can also cause problems in the ministry. This type of person enjoys giving orders and having others obey. He or she rationalizes this tendency by saying, "Well, I am the leader, and leaders must lead. So do what I ask and we'll get the work done." The problem with the authoritarian personality is that people with this trait usually lack sensitivity to other people's feelings. They give goals priority over process, and consequently can easily cause people to feel alienated.

It is important to distinguish here between an authoritarian type of personality and an authoritarian method of leadership. In ministry, there is no one leadership style that should always be preferred over another; the style adopted needs to be tailored to the demands of a particular situation. And authoritarian leadership may sometimes be needed in a crisis situation or when the minister has weak or inept followers (although democratic leadership is almost always better and more effective when the needs of people must be considered), but adopting this style of leadership out of necessity should not be confused with having an authoritarian personality. It is the personality style and not the method of leadership which leads to problems.

The opposite personality trait—underassertiveness—can also cause problems for the minister. Underassertive ministers feel victimized most of the time. They do not know when to stand up for their rights, nor do they have the skills to resist being manipulated by others. In particular, they have great difficulty in saying no and turning down excessive requests for their time. Many ministers with such a personality trait will engage in a lot of fantasy after the event, replaying incidents and rehearsing what they should have said or done in response to being victimized, but the solutions come only in fantasy and are never translated into action. Underassertive ministers feel bullied, beaten, and battered most of the time, and they are only able to claim their rights or stand up for themselves when they have been provoked into anger. When this does happen, however, they are apt to feel they have lost control and their self-respect suffers. Underassertive people usually lack self-esteem and are easily intimidated and manipulated; this produces many loss situations that can lead to depression.

(2) *Ministers may hold unrealistic initial expectations about their work.* Most of us, when about to embark on our careers, have a set of idealized notions about the nature of our intended work. We expect to conquer the world, and we aspire to the highest goals our vocations will allow. For most of us, however, these ambitions will be at least in part unrealized; we will have to learn to trim back our expectations and settle for more modest accomplishments. And this is true in the ministry as well as in other professions. High expectations can turn to disappointment as noble aspirations are tested against the rock of reality.

What sets the ministry apart in this respect, however, is the fact that new pastors and Christian workers tend to have a higher level of idealism than other new professionals; the possibility of disillusionment is therefore even greater. Unfortunately, there is a tendency in churches to overidealize the ministry, and much of this lay stereotyping rubs off on young ministerial candidates.

I see this idealism clearly when I compare two groups I teach at our seminary. The first group is made up of young seminary students intending to become ministers and a few older people planning a career change to the ministry. The second group is made up of Doctor-of-Ministry students who return for seminars after having served a number of years as pastors. The contrast between the two groups is quite revealing. The young students believe that no problem is insurmountable. Solutions flow quickly from their lips during class discussions, and there is even a little resentment expressed if the ministry is not portrayed in an idealized way. The experienced pastors, on the other hand, are more accepting of a realistic analysis of the minister's work. They have begun the painstaking process of revising their unrealistic expectations.

It is inevitable that the idealistic notions a minister or other Christian worker holds at the start of his or her career will change under the influence of experience. The fault is not with the gospel or the spiritual resources available to the pastor, but with the nature of being human. Pastoring is hard work, and somehow it never matches the fantasized images so many start out with. But giving up overidealized notions need not be a negative process. The healthy pastor will work through this process and eventually set aside irrational, unworkable notions. The unhealthy pastor will become disillusioned and pessimistic. Both may experience occasional depression as a result of losing their ideals, but the healthy pastor will grow and become stronger through the experience.

The first five years out of seminary are crucial to the process of revising expectations. I would suggest that during this period every new pastor should be helped by a support group in which he or she can lay bare his or her disappointments and develop a new, healthy set of expectations. A confidential relationship with a more experienced pastor can be helpful—as can supervision by a senior pastor for at least one year after graduation from seminary. This supervising pastor can belong to another church. Many of the problems that can be dealt with in such a supervisory situation transcend denominational or theological boundaries. They are universal because they are the product of the human side of the ministry.

(3) *Many ministers feel conflict over their humanness.* I have found that many ministers and Christian leaders have a haunting suspicion that they are hypocrites. Since they cannot always live up to the high ideals of pastoring or their strongly internalized expectations that they must be exceptional spiritual beings, they often feel that they are failures. In a nutshell, ministers often carry an impossible burden of guilt about their humanness.

The stereotyping of ministers by lay people doesn't help. They often perceive pastors in "nonhuman" terms, even seeing them as a kind of third sex. This forces many ministers to hide their true selves and to conceal weaknesses at all costs. They don't have the privilege of being themselves in all situations, and may develop different facades for different occasions. They may even develop two sides to their personalities—a public one and a private one. Keeping these two sides in harmony by deciding which should be present at any given time becomes a demanding and nerve-racking juggling act that drains energy and easily produces burnout.

To get out of this trap of hypocrisy, some ministers become "hail fellow well-met" types. Instead of hiding their seamy side, they "let it all hang out," putting their negative attributes on public display. They may engage in certain behaviors normally quite foreign to them just to win approval. And they may rationalize such behavior by claiming that they can minister better to people by "getting down on their level" or that it is always better to be "honest" about one's weaknesses.

It is debatable, however, whether becoming so adapted to popular behavior is really effective in reaching people or whether being utterly open about one's weaknesses is really helpful to others. A pastor who lays out his or her dirty linen can easily scare his or her congregation into distrust or even fear. People expect a pastor to be more in control of his or her life than they are of theirs, and so they become insecure when the pastor tries too hard to become "one of the boys."

Even if pastors must avoid the pitfall of trying too hard to seem like everyone else, it is still essential that they come to terms with their humanness and learn to be tolerant of the limits of their frailty. There is not and never has been a sin-proof, temptation-free pastor. We must dispel the notion that God has, in some strange and mysterious way, innoculated the preacher against the disease of sin. And yet this is the cause of many guilt trips that ministers create for themselves. Failure, for them, becomes destructive. It represents loss, and repeated loss of this kind can be a major cause of burnout.

Again and again ministers need to remind themselves that to be human is to be imperfect. God's call to perfection does not mean we are given a shortcut to righteousness, and if we are going to avoid unnecessary depression we must learn how to turn failure into growth and to become courageous in facing our imperfections. As a clinical psychologist, I never cease to marvel at the resources the gospel provides in this area. The concepts, principles, and power of God's message are the most therapeutic forces I know, and when they are used intelligently they can far exceed the puny efforts of psychotherapy alone.

## A Helpful Technique for Understanding a Minister's Loss-Proneness

In order for ministers to improve their ability to cope with job-related burnout and subsequent depression, they need to understand just how likely they are to experience loss as a result of their work. One way to increase awareness of this is to keep a "loss diary" for a short period of time. This practice can be most revealing and can help ministers come to a better understanding of themselves and the unique nature of their work.

To keep a loss diary, a minister writes down, at the end of each day, those experiences that contained elements of loss. It is important to record every loss, no matter how trivial—just the act of recording them can be illuminating.

After a week or so of keeping the diary, the losses should be analyzed. Do they fall into certain categories? Are they concrete, abstract, real, imagined, or threatened losses? If a major loss has been experienced, are there also secondary losses that are related to the larger loss but are harder to recognize? Emotional chaining may have taken place; it is important to identify such chaining and to see how far removed the final emotional state was from the original loss.

In analyzing the loss diary, it is important to look for loss "themes." These are losses which keep repeating themselves. A minister may find, for instance, that he or she consistently takes personal comments as criticisms, or that he or she has an oversensitivity to certain people or events.

The themes identified from the loss diary can be very instructive. One minister may discover, for example, that money issues consistently cause feelings of loss or that lack of material things continually creates insecurity. This may indicate a need to explore the implications of these feelings for his value system and to rethink what is really important in life.

The loss diary may also reveal obvious flaws in communication style. A minister may find that he or she consistently makes too many assumptions about what people will do or fails to obtain confirmation that he or she has been understood, thus leaving his or her communication unclear or ambiguous.

Still another thing the loss diary may reveal is the need to develop compensations in certain areas of life. Ministers may discover they are deficient in certain skills; perhaps his letter writing needs improvement or her sermon delivery could use more zest. Perhaps one minister's administrative skills are poor enough for him to press for the employment of an efficient church business manager. Another minister may need to spend more time with her family.

Systematically examining the loss experiences involved with the work of the ministry through keeping a loss diary can go a long way toward helping ministers cope with or prevent such losses. It can show them areas in their life that need work and can indicate when outside help is needed. And I can think of no better way ministers can inject real meaning into their personal prayer life than providing themselves with accurate information about themselves and their work through such a project. It is my firm belief that God wants us all—ministers included—to progress in our personal growth and sanctification. Bringing our needs to him in a deliberate and focused way can be an important first step in reducing burnout and depression in the ministry.

# 12

## DEPRESSION IN THE MINISTER'S FAMILY

The family is very important to the minister or Christian worker—as it is for most of us. The family serves as a reference or anchoring point, a haven for hassled minds and wearied bodies. It provides confirmation for values, encouragement for labor, a basis for self-identity. It also gives a feeling of belonging and forms the core of all our social ties.

The attitudes of a spouse and children are major factors in determining how satisfied a minister will be in his work. Numerous studies have shown that pastors tend to look to their spouses more than to anyone else to confirm the value of their work. Unmarried ministers may work out a substitute support system, but this is not always satisfying to them. No other relationship provides quite the same level of intimacy or support as the marriage relationship—when it is functioning healthily.

What does this have to do with depression in the ministry? Everything! I do not believe I am exaggerating when I say that it is as hard to live in a family with someone who is depressed as it is to be depressed yourself. The family of a minister who is depressed is going to experience a considerable increase in the stresses and strains of living; it will have difficulty functioning harmoniously. This is also true when the minister's spouse or children are depressed—and this ultimately affects his or her work. I have known some situations in which depression has destroyed a minister's family, or at least produced irreparable damage to its structure!

Fortunately, this does not have to be the case. Depression, like catastrophe in general, can work to unify the members of a minister's family instead of driving them apart. Some families actually become healthier, more caring, and more giving, as a result of the illness.

Whether depression in a minister's family is an experience of devastation and disintegration or one of growth is really a matter of choice. But choosing growth means taking deliberate and planned action for coping with the depression. Neglecting the depression means choosing to let it be destructive. And it takes an exceptional family to *spontaneously* take the right action. Dealing positively with depression in the minister's family takes strategy, effort, and persistence on everyone's part.

## Family Strategies for Turning Depression into Growth

Whether it is the minister or someone else in the family who is suffering from depression, the following steps can help speed healing and help other family members cope with the strain of living with the depressed person (assuming that appropriate treatment is also being carried out):

(1) *At the earliest opportunity, a family conference should be called in which the facts of the depression are frankly discussed and the need for commitment to a determined effort to work it out is stressed.* The nature of this meeting will depend on the age of the children and presence of in-laws or other relations. The spouse of the depressed person may need to take the initiative in calling this conference with family members, since not only will it seem inappropriate for the depressed person to be pleading his or her own cause, but the depression itself will probably make it difficult for him or her to do this.

(2) *At this meeting, and then at other opportune times, family members must be helped to accept the depression as a reality.* At first there may be resistance to this idea, based mainly on ignorance about the depression. Not everyone may be convinced that there is a legitimate problem so a "working through" period may be needed. It is important to emphasize that there is nothing to be gained in fighting or resisting the depression, that depression is not a sign of weakness or inability to cope with life. As we have seen, severe depressions are often endogenous in nature and the sufferer has little or no control over them. Even in the reactive depressions, resisting the normal process will only intensify it. If necessary, family members who are resisting can be persuaded to visit the psychiatrist or psychologist or read a good book on the subject so they can be fully informed of the nature of the depression. The more information they have the easier it will be for them to be patient and understanding.

(3) *The problem must be perceived as a family concern.* The depression is going to have a significant impact on family functioning, so it cannot be ignored. Family members owe it to the depressed member to be cooperative and participate in the healing process.

More primitive cultures can probably teach us a lesson here. In my contact with African culture I have noticed that, even among the most primitive tribes, disease in one member of the family is always considered to be a problem for the whole family. If someone becomes sick, everyone in the family goes to see the doctor. This not only provides tremendous moral support for the sick person but is a concrete acknowledgment of the family's responsibility in the healing process. While in our culture family involvement may be unnecessary in most illnesses, it is absolutely crucial in cases of severe depression. The depression's impact on other family members is so great that they all need to be involved in its treatment!

(4) *Every member of the family must be supportive of the treatment.* So often I find that adolescent children, and even spouses, may send subtle messages of condemnation about the depression and the treatment to the depressed family member. I suspect that this lack of support is usually unconscious and stems from fears of the unknown and our culture's tendency to stigmatize emotional problems. Any hidden resistance of this kind to the treatment should be brought into the open, confronted, and disposed of. Depressed people are doubtful enough about whether they are doing the right thing without others raising additional suspicions and negative feelings.

(5) *Ways should be found to reduce resentment.* Chances are that a depression will be resented by close family members. No one wants to be around a person who is dejected, negative, critical, uncooperative, and withdrawn, and this is how the depressed family member will be perceived. It is important that everyone understand that these are *symptoms* of the depression and should not be taken personally. Instead, the depressed person should be treated with kindness, patience, and long-suffering. If 1 Corinthians 13 has not meant anything personal to family members before, it should now. The depressed person will need to feel loved, accepted, and understood if healing is to take place and guilt over being depressed is to be minimized.

(6) *Family responsibilities should be rearranged for the duration of the depression.* This may require an older child's assuming responsibility for maintaining the car or taking care of the garden. Others may have to take over the remaining chores. Pressure to attend school functions, Little League, conduct family devotions, or other regular responsibilities, should be reduced. This is not really bad, since parents tend not to give responsibility to children soon enough, anyway. In this respect, the depression may be a blessing because it provides an opportunity for talent and skills to be developed.

(7) *The family (including the spouse) should then be encouraged to go about its business normally.* This does not mean they must ignore or

neglect the depressed person, but life must go on and the presence of depression, no matter how incapacitating, should not be allowed to disrupt more of life than is absolutely necessary. The rest of the family should spend time with the depressed person, but not be dominated by his or her needs.

(8) *Last, the depressed person will need much prayer and spiritual support through this difficult time.* Often depressed people do not feel like praying or reading Scripture for themselves, and the reassurance that those who love them will be praying with and for them can keep hope alive. Prayer during this time should be very specific and should be directed toward the *problem* and not the *person*. Since the depressed person is very vulnerable to guilt feelings at this time, any comments that could be construed as criticism or condemnation should be avoided. God's Spirit can be trusted to convict the depressed person when it is necessary; there is no reason other people should feel called on to do that job themselves.

## Can a Spouse Be a Therapist?

I am often asked whether the spouse of a depressed person can act as a therapist of sorts. My answer is simple: It depends on the spouse and the nature of the marriage relationship. However, rarely have I found it possible for a spouse to serve as the exclusive therapist to a depressed partner, even when the spouse is a trained counselor.

Don't misunderstand me. Much therapeutic healing *does* take place in a marriage relationship. A sympathetic, understanding, and communicative spouse is very helpful to someone experiencing depression. But he or she is still an "interested" party and very affected by the depression. It is hard for anyone in such a position to be objective. Very intimate feelings shared with a wife (or husband) can, in a moment of anger at a later time, be turned and used as a weapon. This ends all therapeutic effects. The role of therapist or counselor requires much impartiality and is fundamentally in conflict with the role of the spouse.

This is one of the reasons why I cannot be a therapist to my own family. I will often say to them, "I will not play psychologist at home. I want the privilege of being myself and, if necessary, of becoming emotional and erratic when those I love do things that cause me hurt or threaten their own happiness. Don't expect me to remain as objective and impartial as I am with my patients. While I will gladly give my advice when it is appropriate (and occasionally at other times also), I want you to love me for being the imperfect father and husband that I am—not for being a therapist."

The spouse of a depressed person can try to do many things that a therapist does—but it just doesn't work to try to be impartial. A depressed person needs someone else who can fulfill this role—an objective party with whom deepest feelings can be shared. The fact that he or she cannot share these feelings with the spouse does not mean they do not have an intimate marriage. The kinds of feelings that are revealed in therapy are often transitory and elusive; the only purpose in bringing them to light is to open the way to better self-understanding. This is usually most effectively done with a third party whose own feelings aren't closely involved.

## When the Minister's Spouse Is Depressed

There are many reasons why a minister's spouse can become depressed. Some of these are related to the interaction between the family and the minister's vocation, some to personal tensions between the minister and the spouse, some to endogenous or physical factors. The steps listed above for turning depression into growth are extremely helpful in these cases, but there are other issues which may need to be understood if healing is to take place.

The depression of a spouse can have a debilitating effect on the pastor. He or she will have to compensate for the spouse's diminished activity and will also be subjected to much additional stress. The spouse may use the minister as a scapegoat and blame his work for the way he or she feels. Or the minister, on the other hand, may not be very understanding of the depression and may demand more from the spouse than he or she can provide. In such a situation the potential for conflict and misunderstanding is extremely high.

One very sad case I once treated concerned a minister who had married his childhood sweetheart. After graduating from seminary he began his ministry with a strong sense of God's calling. After their first child was born the wife began experiencing periodic depression. They did not discuss these depressions with anyone else, because they feared others would see them as a sign of weakness; they also expected these bouts with depression would go away. After a while, however, these periodic depressions began to cause tension in the home. The husband would expect his wife to attend a function and she would refuse to go, stating that she "wasn't feeling well." He increased the pressure on her to "be normal" and she retaliated by blaming him and his work for her unhappy feelings. After four years of this, they eventually sought my help.

I worked with them for a while but could not convince the wife that her depression, though now aggravated by the demands and expectations of her pastor-husband, had an underlying endogenous component and needed to be treated with medication. She insisted that her depression was her husband's fault and that he needed to change. He gave it a try, and after a year of psychotherapy he *had* changed considerably. He was less demanding and had come to terms with his pride and the "image" he wanted his wife to project. But she remained unchanged; she continued experiencing depression and rejecting him because of it. Nothing could shake her from her rigid position.

Shortly afterwards they moved to another part of the country, and two years later they were divorced—all because the wrong cause was blamed for the depression.

## The Unique Emotional Hazards the Minister's Family Faces

The pastor's family is subjected to a unique set of emotional hazards. Some of these can be avoided but some cannot. In either case, careful planning and intelligent problem solving can minimize many of the adverse effects. Among the unique hazards that may predispose the minister's family (and especially the spouse) to conflicts and possible depression are:

(1) *The minister's work and family life are closely intertwined.* I know of no occupation in which the spouse is as intimately involved in the work of his or her partner as in the ministry. The typical church, for example, holds a strong expectation for the minister's wife or husband to be part of the ministry. The minister's family life is an important professional criterion to be evaluated when he or she is being considered for employment and when work is being reviewed. There is hardly anything the minister does that doesn't have an impact on the family and vice versa. In fact, some ministerial spouses come to feel that they are married to the church as well as to the minister, and children feel they are literally "growing up in the church."

This mutual involvement and interdependence between the minister's work and the minister's family can be a tremendous boon, but it can also be a source of tension, conflict, and depression. When depression does occur, it can often be aggravated by the intertwining of work and personal life. Another problem that may develop as a consequence of the whole family's receiving a clergy-defined role is that they may be driven into a mutual dependence so strong that the members of the family fail to develop other reference and support systems. This can put undue strain on family relationships.

(2) *The family is constantly on display.* Every step of every member of the pastor's family is likely to be closely scrutinized (if only out of curiosity) and criticism leveled at any deviation from the expected

behavior. This standard of behavior is usually higher than that expected of everyone else in the church; the pastor's family is expected to maintain a higher level of spirituality than everyone else. Church members often feel that certain kinds of behavior are acceptable for *them* but unacceptable for the minister's spouse and children; this double standard can cause much resentment in the minister's family—especially on the part of the children.

Unfortunately, the minister may also buy into these expectations from the congregation—often without being aware of it—and this can impose a strain on normal family functioning. In such instances father or mother becomes a policeman, guarding against infringements on congregational expectations and inflicting punishment to enforce compliance. One pastor's son said to me, "I hate my father for always forcing me to behave so as to please his congregation." That father may have won a congregation—but he lost a son!

(3) *The pastor's spouse especially is subjected to a set of role expectations from the church.* In churches where the pastor is male (still the vast majority), the wife is subject to special expectations. If she accepts these she can be quite happy and fulfilled. But if she doesn't fit into the expected role and fails to negotiate alternatives, she can be constantly miserable!

Not all these role expectations are reasonable; in fact, some may be absolutely archaic. For instance, in some churches there is an unwritten rule that the pastor's wife must attend all church functions, that she must always be the chairperson for the ladies' group, that she must not have a career outside of her marriage, that she must always open her home to everyone who wants to visit, and that she must always keep her house cleaner and tidier than everyone else.

While these notions seem ridiculous when we look at them presented this way, there are untold numbers of pastors' wives who accept them and live them out. Many pay for it in resentment and depression.

(4) *Most pastors' families suffer from financial problems.* It is a sad indictment of Christian work that, with few exceptions, it expects its servants to work for very much less than what would be considered a fair wage for comparable work in the secular world. This can cause much unfair hardship for the families of ministers and Christian workers. The struggle to survive and to provide one's family with reasonable amenities can be a major source of conflict between spouses and children. It is often a cause for depression.

(5) *The unreliability of the time a pastor spends with his family is counterproductive to family growth and unity.* Pastors' wives usually don't complain about the *amount* of time their husbands spend with the family as much as they complain about the fact that time spent with the

family is *unpredictable*. Frequent emergencies, inability to say no to requests, unexpected changes in schedules, and failure to place family priorities high enough are common reasons for this problem. I've known pastors to cancel a holiday planned a year in advance because some "more important" church business came up. More frequently, family outings or evenings at home are ruined. Small wonder the family comes to feel that they always play "second fiddle" to the minister's work.

The unreliability of ministers' time often makes their spouses strong candidates for depression. They feel trapped—after all, it is "the Lord's work." Who are they to object? Should they not sacrifice their needs for the sake of the congregation? Meanwhile, they worry about how to explain this to their deeply disappointed children, unsure that they really accept this evaluation themselves.

In many pastors' households this unacceptable situation comes to be symbolized by the intrusive and always-ringing telephone. Of all the instruments of destruction humankind has invented, the telephone must be the greatest—for the pastor's spouse, at least. Many ministerial wives and husbands come to hate the telephone. It interrupts family togetherness, intrudes at the most inappropriate times, and takes the pastor away, even though he or she is still at home. Often the phone becomes a cue for depression. "If the telephone rings while we are having dinner I go into a deep depression and remain that way for hours," one wife told me.

## Minimizing the Hazards of Ministry for the Family

Much can be done toward preventing these hazards from creating or aggravating depression. I suggest the following:

(1) *A minister can educate his or her congregation about the roles of family members,* clarifying those roles which the spouse and children do not wish to adopt. He should explain how easy it is for a congregation to place demands on the family that are based on experiences with previous pastors' families and may not fit them. He or she can also show how stereotypes can operate to perpetuate erroneous ideas and how this can create a strain on normal growth and development.

I believe almost every congregation is basically open to being educated on these issues. They *do* want to understand and help. (If not, there are other serious problems involved and the congregation's pressure on the minister's family is basically a message of rejection. Such attitudes may be good reason for a move to a new church.) Such educating can easily be incorporated into sermon illustrations which use family incidents or by hosting special "family evenings" in which the minister and his or her family share themselves with the congregation. A male minister's wife can be given an opportunity to share her feelings with significant women in her group. Even the church bulletin can be used to provide personal "cameos" of family members and clarify their roles.

It is especially important that ministers and their spouses clarify roles and expectations when they are interviewed for a new church position. If what is expected of the minister's family is unacceptable, then a change should be negotiated. It is better to do this *before* accepting a position, since it can be most depressing for a minister and spouse to find out "after the fact" that they are expected to do something they don't want to do. Young pastors seeking their first church are probably the most reluctant to check out expectations before taking any appointment. This can spell trouble.

(2) *The minister can protect the family from being put on display or being subjected to unreasonable demands.* It is important to ensure that the family feels the freedom to be themselves. This is not a matter of giving children license to do whatever they want, but more an attitude of accepting the normal phases of development and coming to terms with fear of what your congregation may think. Unconditional love and acceptance are always the most effective attitudes for child rearing.

(3) *The minister can involve his or her spouse in personal growth and development and in whatever other activities he or she would like.* A male pastor in particular should encourage his wife to be her own self, to discover her own hidden talents, to use her gifts, and to choose what aspects of the ministry in which she wants to be involved. A loving spouse will provide her opportunities to serve and provide protection from trivia so there is *time* for her to serve.

In many ministerial families, the wife's education has been cut short in favor of the husband's. It is easy for the pastor to outgrow his spouse both intellectually and in maturity and thus remove a common basis for interaction. To counteract this tendency, the minister should encourage his spouse in her education. Whether this is undertaken formally through a local college or seminary, or informally through reading on her own, the minister's spouse needs to feel that she is growing and developing her skills and knowledge. This will make her feel more confident about her own worth and the contribution she can make.

(4) *It's best to be assertive in the area of money.* Congregations are not always unreasonable; sometimes they merely lack adequate information. Assertiveness is better and healthier than resentment. The minister should be open and honest about the family's living expenses and the struggles they are having. It is better to deal with the issue once, and deal with it properly, than to go back every five or six months

and ask for a little more. Regular salary reviews and cost-of-living increases should be negotiated, and a committee set up to handle these matters and present the minister's case. A well-informed committee is a good protection against suspicions that the minister may be distorting his or her needs.

It cannot be sufficiently stressed how important this step is in ensuring that the minister and his or her spouse do not develop conscious or unconscious resentment towards the church. Most ministers are reluctant to talk about money matters; they feel it is "unspiritual" and possibly a sign of inadequate faith. But this is hardly a faith issue. "Ye have not, because ye ask not" is as much a practical principle as it is a matter of faith. It applies as much to human relationships as it does to our relationship with God.

(5) *The minister must give primacy to spouse and family.* It is irrational for a minister to perceive the family as being in competition with his or her service to God. The minister's family *is* a part of his or her ministry. It's important not to fall into the trap of believing that a minister who gives the family attention is neglecting the ministry. Paul makes it very clear in 1 Timothy 3:4–5 that a minister (or elder) must "manage his own family well" (NIV). If ministers cannot do this, how can they care for God's church? If they fail to fulfill their responsibilities to their families, they fail to fulfill their responsibilities as ministers of the gospel!

(6) *It's important to deal with problems of loneliness, especially in the minister's spouse.* Although this is beginning to change, many pastors' wives do not have close friends or a support group. They feel isolated, don't always like the people in their congregation, and often are preoccupied with rearing their children. Some of them have tried making close friends with congregational members, only to find that they are always "set apart" and viewed as different. When they have shared intimate and personal details of their life as a pastor's wife, those confidences have been violated or the pastor's effectiveness has been diminished. It may be necessary, therefore, for a minister's wife to seek friendships with compatible women from other church groups or with other ministers' wives.

It is a fallacy to think that friendship must be confined to those who believe *exactly* as we do. While the minister's wife probably would not find any common basis for friendship with someone who is not a Christian, there are many potential friends available in other churches. This "cross-fertilizing" of friendship may even be beneficial. My wife has found it very helpful to be in a prayer group with women who do not attend the same church as we do. In fact, each member attends a different church. This has provided a rich source of ideas and insights for her personal growth that she probably would not have experienced if she were being exposed only to her regular circle of church friends.

## Some Ministers Increase the Depression Hazards for Their Families

While the minister's family is subject to a unique set of hazards which are likely to both create as well as aggravate depression, no discussion would be complete without commenting on how some pastors tend to produce depression in their families. There are some ministers who are so caught up in their work and have such a strong need to avoid failure or please congregations that they become unreasonable in the demands they make on their families. Such pastors can actually be "pathogenic agents"—they can create unhappiness and produce neuroses, including depression, in their families.

Such pastors think their demands are very reasonable. They want to be the best pastors they can be. They want their families to be involved in the ministry in as many ways as possible. They believe that what they want from their spouses and children is in the families' best interest also. But they are also very insecure, unsure of themselves, and afraid that they are not making it as ministers. So they demand from their families total compliance and conformity to what they perceive that the church wants, or to what they believe will make their ministry most effective.

These demands will seldom be enforced with affection or tenderness. Usually such pastors are cold and distant, almost paranoid in their demands. They will be suspicious of what their spouses and children are doing behind their backs, and whenever they want compliance they use their power in an autocratic, domineering way to achieve it.

Needless to say, fear is the predominant mood of such a family. At first, the fear breeds anxiety and the children may show this in a variety of ways: nail-biting, nervousness, upset stomach, and frequent pouting. The spouse may react by becoming overly protective of the children and avoiding all open hostility. After a while he or she may develop such physical responses to stress as headaches, ulcers, or colitis. Depression, often in its low-grade and persistent form, is very common in both the children and the spouse in these situations.

Later, as the children reach adolescence, the fear may turn to resentment. They resent the demands placed on them. They resent being neglected. The only real contact they have with their minister parent is when they are being hassled over issues of compliance. They resent having to listen to sermons over issues they know are not practiced by

138

the pastor. In short, they carry all the signs of a resentment that is usually the byproduct of a love-deprived and overdemanding upbringing. They become the neurotic byproducts of a pathogenic pastor.

If you are such a pastor, then you need to change. You may be deeply insecure and unsure of yourself. Your self-esteem may be too low or you may be incapable of intimacy, so you "love from a distance." These problems are deep-seated and, while simply being aware of them (so you can pray more intelligently about the problem) can bring about some change, psychotherapy may be the more effective and permanent way of exploring and rectifying them.

## Depression in the Pastor's Children

Depressive reactions will not necessarily be confined just to the pastor and his or her spouse. The problems of the ministry can carry over to the children also and give rise to reactions which many times will *not* be recognized as depression. Children do not always show depression in quite the same way as adults. This has led some researchers to insist that adult models of depression are not directly applicable to children. My experience has been that, while children experience the same *causes* as do adults, the *symptoms* of their depressions are sometimes different. Because of their more limited life experience and slightly different physiology, children often show depression as rebellion, negativity, resentment, and anger. The feature which most parallels the adult experience is social isolation and withdrawal, and in the child this is often the predominant symptom. The child goes to his room and avoids all contacts. He appears worried or preoccupied and will not engage in conversation or explain what is bothering him.

A composite picture of the depressed child, based on our present state of knowledge of the dominant symptoms, would be as follows:

(1) *The child presents a sad, unhappy appearance, but does not complain of unhappiness or even exhibit awareness of it.* He seems to "slow down" both physically and psychologically.

(2) *The child loses interest in all activities,* gives the impression of being bored or sick; this may lead the parent to suspect there is a concealed physical illness.

(3) *The child begins to exhibit physical complaints* such as headaches, abdominal discomfort, insomnia, and eating disturbances.

(4) *The child appears discontented, and gives the impression that little pleasure can be experienced.* He may blame others for this and feel rejected or unloved.

(5) *A low frustration tolerance creates irritability.* When goals are

not accomplished, the child engages in self-rejection, self-punishment, and negative self-statements.

(6) *The child may periodically engage in "acting-out" behavior* as a defense against experiencing the painful feelings associated with depression. These behaviors can take the form of mistreating younger siblings, temper tantrums, lying, stealing, getting into trouble at school, and general misbehaving.

## Helping a Child's Depression

Since in nearly all reactive depressions a loss of some sort has taken place, searching for apparent losses and identifying them for your child can help to relieve the depression. The child should be approached with specific questions such as: "Did anything special happen to you today?" or "Tell me about school. How is your teacher?"

These questions should be designed to elicit *facts* about the child's life—*not* feelings. Children usually have difficulty describing feelings. In fact, approaching a child with questions such as: "What's wrong with you; why are you so down?" or "Why do you feel the way you do?" is only likely to cause more withdrawal. Not only are these questions condemning to the child (they imply something is wrong with him), but they require the child to be able to explain why he feels the way he does—a skill the average child has not yet learned and will resent being asked to do.

Many childhood losses are imagined or threatened. The child fears such things as his parents' reaction to poor school performance (the loss of parental respect), rejection from peers (the loss of friendship and self-respect), and bad things that may happen in the future (the loss of security). Many of these losses are the product of inadequately developed minds. Children don't yet know enough to be able to understand the complexities of life, nor have they experienced enough to be able to predict the outcome of life events. Often all that it takes to resolve the depression is to reassure the child and place whatever real loss has occurred in its proper perspective.

Unfortunately, not all childhood depressions are reactive. Researchers report that, while endogenous depressions are not as common among children as among adults, there is a clearly defined group of endogenously depressed youngsters whose depressions are generally not recognized and who could benefit from antidepressant medication. Such children are at high risk for adult depression; genetic and biochemical factors predispose them to depression at an early age and this can carry over to the adult years. Therefore, any child who experiences depression regularly or who is depressed without cause should be carefully evaluated by a mental health professional. A family physician can be the starting point; he can perform a number of standard tests to ensure that the endocrine system (especially the thyroid) is functioning normally and that there are no other physiological causes or problems underlying the depression.

Since much can be done to prevent the development of patterns of behavior that could predispose the child to depression later in life, psychotherapy should be sought if a persistent problem exists. Prevention is much better than cure, and many potential triggers to depression can be defused in the childhood years.

## Preventing Depression in the Minister's Family

There is much that a minister or Christian worker can do to prevent depression in his or her family. Careful analysis of the circumstances that seem to upset the other family members should provide him or her with the insights needed to take corrective steps.

Some causes of depression are common to *all* families, some apply only to the families of pastors, and some are very specific to a particular pastor's family. Here are some important ways in which a minister can either remedy or avoid depression in his or her family:

(1) *Avoid using the family as a scapegoat.* It's important for the minister to identify the *real* sources of his or her anger, anxiety, and frustration and to direct attention there. If possible all feelings of hostility and frustration that arise from work should be resolved *before* going home to the family. If they cannot be resolved, then they should be left at the office and not inflicted on the family.

(2) *Give the family permission to be themselves.* It's crucial to encourage communication over points of conflict or feelings of pressure from you. This is the only way the minister can know the ways the family is being negatively influenced.

(3) *Establish clear guidelines for behavior,* but only in dialogue with family members. Participative planning always maximizes cooperation. The family usually understands the position the pastor is in and is willing to assist in accomplishing clearly understood objectives. But they have rights also, and these need to be given equal consideration.

(4) *Develop compensation for the losses the family will naturally suffer because their spouse or parent is a minister.* There are many things a pastor can do to provide the family with some reasonable alternatives for the luxuries their peers may have or the privileges they may be missing. Often a happy and loving home environment can

compensate for many material losses. But families can also find many hobbies and interests that can build feelings of togetherness and security with little demand on income.

(5) *Build their self-esteem by unconditional positive regard.* The minister's power to make or break the family's spirit should not be underestimated. Perhaps he or she needs to begin by building his or her own self-esteem; a person who is negative about himself or herself and who has a distorted self-image can hardly provide the realistic and honest feedback that is needed to build a healthy self-esteem in other family members. By building the self-esteem of spouse and children, the minister will be doing two important things that will be helpful in preventing depression. First, he or she will be teaching them not to be devastated by failure, since who they are as persons will not be dependent upon what they do. Second, he or she will be teaching them that forgiveness, especially self-forgiveness, is always healthier than self-punishment.

# 13

## BUILDING RESISTANCE TO
## DEPRESSION

One of the most liberating and therapeutic discoveries of my own personal growth has been the realization that I can build resistance to depression. Just as my body can build up immunity to harmful microbes and bacteria, my mind can be strengthened to resist depression.

True, there are those depressions which cannot be avoided. There are many legitimate losses in life and it is appropriate to grieve over them. This is how God has designed us. Failure to cooperate with his intelligent purpose in the working of our minds and bodies will only lead to these natural processes' becoming destructive. But is every loss a true loss? Is it possible that a life event we perceive as catastrophic can, in fact, turn out to be a blessing from God?

I could relate many stories of cases where the apparent catastrophic loss of either a job or prized possession has turned out to be the means of greater blessing. I remember a married man of thirty who came to see me on referral from his pastor. He had started a business four or five years before and, to raise enough capital, had borrowed money from his own parents, his wife's parents, and a number of church members. At first the business thrived. But then, due to a number of uncontrollable economic factors, things went bad for the man. Within a week he was bankrupt and went into a deep depression. He blamed himself for borrowing from relatives and friends and hid away from them out of shame.

In my office his message to me was very straight. "If you can't help me quickly to straighten out my depression, I am going to kill myself. I cannot face my wife, family, or friends." I began to talk to this man about his values and the difference between those aspects of life that have eternal significance and those that do not. I listened to his pathetic story and tried to show him that everything he was concerned about had no eternal consequence. He was very attentive and responsive. I knew God was confirming my message to him.

He agreed to see me every day for a period of time, and by the fifth day I began to see a change. He took control of his catastrophe, shook himself out of his state of helplessness, courageously handled all the details of closing down his business, and began to resolve his relationships with those whose money he had borrowed. No miracles happened! He did not suddenly recover from his financial disaster. But during this period he received a clear call from God to missionary service. Within months he began his training and today he and his wife are on the mission field. Just before he left for overseas service he wrote to me and said, "My business failure was *not* a disaster. Out of it came the greatest blessing anyone can experience—I found what God wanted me to do with my life."

Just being aware of the fact that blessing can often be hidden in catastrophe can be helpful in building our tolerance for depression. If we straighten out our values and keep our life perspective close to God's, I do believe we *can* build resistance to much depression. We do not bypass loss, but we develop a *perspective* on loss that prevents unnecessary grieving or accelerates the natural grieving process. In some circumstances, just the acknowledgement that a loss of a certain kind has occurred is sufficient to place it in perspective. No further grieving is then necessary.

Building resistance to depression takes discipline and, if a person has developed the habit of deriving satisfaction from being depressed, it also takes a sacrificing of these benefits. In the long run, however, making the effort to build resistance pays off. Pastors and Christian workers owe it to themselves and to their ministries not to be incapacitated by unnecessary or frequent depression.

## Learn from Past Depression

Many depressions repeat themselves over and over again. The same incident, or word of criticism, or misperceived motive, or implied rejection, or unfulfilled expectation can trigger depression over and over without the depressed person's ever learning how to benefit from it and how to avoid future depression.

One pastor's wife told me how she always became depressed when her husband came home at the end of the day. Her complaint was that he did not show his affection to her by kissing her before doing anything else. I asked her, "How many times in your twenty years of marriage has he forgotten to kiss you when he arrives home?" She replied that he always went straight for the newspaper.

"Have you ever asked him to kiss you before he does anything else?" I pressed. "No, that would mean that his affection was not spontaneous," was her reply.

And so this woman had gone on being depressed over an expectation of her own creation which had never been communicated to her husband, and which had never been fulfilled in all her years of married life. She had experienced regular depression and had not learned how to prevent it. During our discussion, however, she realized how she was creating her depression. She went home and opened communication with her husband about her feelings. And from what I've heard he now always gives her a kiss when he arrives home—and they both enjoy it!

There are many ways in which a specific trigger can set off repeated depressions and still elude recognition. The use of a "loss diary" as described in a previous chapter can help to identify such a trigger and can also reveal persistent tendencies either to interpret events as losses when none really exists or to exaggerate small losses. Such a technique will quickly see whether the problem is one of assertiveness, cowardice, over-confidence, or overemotionalizing. The individual's values and perspective on life will readily become apparent, because there is nothing like depression to show a person "where his heart is." A minister may be very surprised to discover what it is he tends to treasure.

Whether a minister uses the technique of a "loss diary" or simply reflects on past depressions, learning from depression should be a high priority. And making the effort to analyze past depressions can also lead to a very important discovery—perhaps there is an endogenous form of depression involved that should be receiving treatment.

## Each Person Should Understand His or Her Own Physiology

Just as each individual's mind and personality are distinctive and unique, each one of us has a physiology unlike anyone else's. For this reason, we each have a characteristic way of experiencing depression; different individuals differ in their susceptibility to its symptoms. Some will have a greater predisposition to fatigue and adrenal exhaustion and will, therefore, experience tiredness when they are depressed. Some will experience a lowered tolerance for stress and will therefore find themselves in states of distress that can aggravate depression.

Since no two people are alike, it is pointless for one person to drive himself or herself to perform at the level at which he or she thinks others function. This has been the downfall of many ministers. "But my senior pastor can put in twelve hours a day, why can't I?" is a very common response of younger ministers. But the senior pastor may be a very unusual person with enormous reserves of energy and a high tolerance for stress. Or he may not actually be working as hard as it seems; he may take numerous breaks and know when to rest.

My message here is very simple: If we abuse our bodies through overwork, lack of adequate rest, and too much stress, we will pay for it in depression. Such depressions are not mysterious, and there's no need to dig for deep underlying psychological causes. The solution is just to slow down! Heeding the messages of the body and accepting the limitations of one's particular physiology can eliminate a lot of unnecessary depression.

I concede that coming to understand the limitations and unique responsiveness of an individual physiology requires some determined and disciplined effort, but the dividends are great. I would suggest a person begin by increasing the attention given to the body—not in the hypochondriac sense of focusing on all its pains and discomforts, but in the sense of understanding how it functions. He should pay particular attention to how it draws on adrenalin and responds to anxiety and stress. Such knowledge can help him predict a feeling of "let down" after a period of excitement or sustained effort and plan his schedule to allow adequate recovery time.

The body's resources for dealing with depression can be increased by improving the body's tolerance for anxiety and stress. Two basic steps I would suggest are:

(1) *Eating a proper diet and exercising regularly.* These are great protections against disease. Our Western lifestyle is far too sedentary, and the "running around" we do when we work is too stressful to be of any real benefit. Exercising should take place in a stress-free environment so that while fatigue of the muscle systems is being produced, other systems can turn off. Exercise should take place on a *daily* basis and be tailored to your age and physical condition.

(2) *Learning a relaxation technique.* In the past few years our culture has rediscovered the power of relaxation. The emphasis on "resting" and the concept of the Sabbath in Scripture, particularly the Old Testament, is not surprising to a contemporary stress researcher. In fact much of my clinical research and work is devoted to teaching effective relaxation through the monitoring of certain physiological systems. Known as "biofeedback," these techniques are very effective in treating stress-related disorders such as tension and migraine headaches.

How can a busy minister learn effective relaxation? A relaxation technique often used by clinicians is known as "progressive relaxation." It can be coupled with spiritual exercises such as prayer and Christian meditation and thus serve as a spiritual exercise also. A person who wants to practice this technique begins by lying in a comfortable position on a couch or bed that provides support to all parts of the body. Starting with the toes, and moving progressively up the body, he begins a process of first tensing a muscle for five seconds, then relaxing it and keeping it immobile as the next muscle is tensed. This process of first producing a slight fatigue by tensing the muscle, then leaving it totally inactive, continues until every muscle in the body has been used. Then the person should remain in this inactive state for twenty or thirty minutes but *not* go to sleep. After five or six such relaxation exercises his residual muscle tension will begin to go down. If it doesn't, he should seek professional help.

## Learning Assertive Behavior

Much reactive depression is the consequence of feeling out of control and victimized by other people. Ministers, because of the large numbers of people with whom they relate, often feel that they are being controlled by others. This leads to resentment and anger, a loss of self-respect, and depression. Unfortunately, instead of developing a healthy assertive response, many ministers with this problem either become aggressive and make the mistake of using anger to achieve their needs, or passively resign themselves to circumstances. Either way, they are in trouble.

There is much confusion in Christian circles about what constitutes a healthy assertiveness and how one can be assertive and still be Christlike. So I want to begin by clearly defining what assertiveness is and by drawing a distinction between "Christian assertiveness," and the popular secular ideas of assertiveness.

I believe that there is an appropriate and healthy form of Christian assertiveness which is compatible with New Testament teachings on self-sacrifice, the avoidance of self-seeking, and the danger of self-glorification. Unfortunately, many Christians have developed a rationalization for their underassertiveness. They erroneously call their inability to stand up for themselves "Christian humility." But Christian humility and love are *not* intended to be a cover for cowardice. Paul Tournier expresses this fact well in his book, *A Place for You*, (New York: Harper & Row, 1968) when he says, "Christians practice self-denial prematurely" (p. 125). He goes on to say that many Christians deny themselves before they possess themselves, and thus confuse self-denial with self-depreciation.

For ministers, the consequence of this confusion is that they do not know how or when to be assertive. They become the victims of manipulation by others, unable to confront destructive forces and afraid to say no for fear of losing the respect of others. The only time they can stand up for their legitimate rights is when they are pushed into anger, and the eruption that follows only serves to alienate people further.

Unlike some secular interpretations of assertiveness, "Christian assertiveness" does *not* place the individual's rights *above* the rights of others. It does not require that a person always stand up for himself, and it makes room for him to sacrifice his rights when circumstances require it. But there are many situations that arise in the lives of ministers that require strong positive responses—times when they need to protect their families, advance the work of the kingdom of God, and avoid becoming angry and depressed. In times like this a healthy Christian assertiveness is in order.

Healthy assertiveness means, very simply, that people can stand up for themselves without feeling guilty, refuse to let others manipulate them or impose their wills on them, express their feelings in a non-hostile manner, refuse to be intimidated, and confront conflict courageously. People with a healthy assertiveness don't feel the need to apologize continually for making mistakes, and do not engage in fantasizing "after the event" what they should have done. They stand up to aggressive people and authority figures without being intimidated. And they do all this in a calm, loving, objective manner—*without* becoming angry or abusive.

Such assertive behavior *is* compatible with a Christian spirit when it is done in love and with respect toward others. It is the way of honesty and openness—a way ministers can become the real people God has called them to be. Learning a healthy assertiveness can help ministers improve communication with others, get them out of a state of helplessness, and free them from a pervasive sense of frustration.

## Improving Assertiveness

How can a minister learn to be more assertive? A full treatment of the topic goes well beyond the limits of this book but, briefly, learning assertiveness requires two steps:

(1) *Improving self-attitudes*. A change of attitude must precede the practice of assertiveness. Individuals must convince themselves that they have the right to be themselves. This is not to rob others of their rights, but to enable them both as persons and as pastors to do God's work and to be faithful to his calling. Their goal should not be to dominate others, but to claim the freedom to be themselves.

It's important to remember that Jesus himself was assertive. He stood up to the Pharisees and resisted Satan. When his time came, he surrendered his body to the cross—but not because he had no choice!

148

He went to his death not because he was a coward who couldn't resist group pressure, but because he chose of his *own free will* to do so. His followers have this *same freedom* to make their own decisions and act on them.

(2) *Practicing assertiveness.* Once a person's attitude is right, practice will establish the appropriate habits of assertiveness. It's probably a good idea for a minister to start slowly, keeping in mind always that the goal of assertiveness is freedom to be oneself. Ministers can begin to practice assertiveness by saying no to invitations they don't want to accept and by resisting the temptation to give lengthy explanations or excuses; after all, it *is* their right to decide. Giving compliments to others, starting conversations with strangers, questioning the check at restaurants (when it's in doubt!), requesting adjustment when services are not rendered properly, returning the car for further repairs if the work was not done satisfactorily, voicing an objection when someone "cuts into" a line—all these can be valuable exercises for underassertive ministers in "stretching" themselves to full stature as persons.

If behaviors like these are carried out politely and *without* anger, most people will welcome them; they prefer openness and honesty. The minister will feel better for having stood up for himself or herself, and as a result he or she will become more flexible, adaptable, and sensitive to the feelings of others. Most important, he or she will be developing feelings of confidence, personal worth, and respect for others, and will avoid going through life feeling devalued and inhibited. He or she will be building resistance to depression by developing the skills needed to escape from depression-producing circumstances.

For further reading about this important subject, let me suggest two excellent books. The first is *Your Perfect Right: A Guide to Assertive Living* by Robert E. Alberti and Michael L. Emmons (San Luis Obispo, CA: Impact Pubs., 1982). It is not written from a Christian perspective, but is nevertheless very sound. The second is *Anger and Assertiveness in Pastoral Care* (Philadelphia: Fortress Press, 1979) by David Augsburger, a highly respected Christian writer.

## Correcting Patterns of Thinking

Clear and rational thinking helps to avoid unnecessary depression. This idea is thoroughly biblical. Proverbs 23:7 reminds us that "as he thinketh in his heart, so *is* he," and it is Paul's advice that we should "let this mind be in you, which was also in Christ Jesus" (Phil. 2:5). Later in this Epistle he encourages us to think about things that are true, honest, just, pure, lovely, and of good report (Phil. 4:8). Why? Because if we think about these things we will become like them.

A more complete treatment of how important thoughts are in determining emotions is given in chapter 3 of my book, *Feeling Free*. For the purposes of this book, however, I simply wish to draw attention to four thinking styles that tend to increase depression proneness:

(1) *Catastrophic thinking*. This is a tendency to make catastrophes out of normal life events. It is the consequence of experiencing too much anxiety. When we think this way, the threat of losing some prized object or opportunity or its actual loss causes so much discomfort that the loss is viewed as irreplaceable. Catastrophic thinking makes things seem worse than they really are.

This penchant for overdramatizing and seeing only the negative or catastrophic side of life is, of course, a characteristic of our age. Movies, television, and the newspaper media thrive on catastrophic headlines and circumstances. This tends to warp our interpretation of normal events.

To catastrophize means to take relatively minor life events and blow them out of proportion. For example, let us suppose I am driving to a speaking engagement at a local Rotary Club meeting. On the way I have a flat tire. I pull over to the side of the road, get out of the car, and look mournfully at the flat. I interpret what has happened as "terrible" and "awful," and ask, "Why does this always happen to me?" In essence, I create a catastrophe out of the event. My anxiety about being late causes me to distort the seriousness of the event, and a panic reaction is very likely to set in. In my panic I may become careless and ineffective, and the chances are that I will botch the tire change and not make the appointment at all. In contrast, a calm, objective, non-catastrophic response maximizes the efficiency with which I can correct the unfortunate (but not catastrophic) event.

Cognitive psychologists emphasize that humans do not *get* upset, but *upset themselves*. They do this by devoutly convincing themselves that (1) whatever happens has no right to happen in the first place, and (2) nothing can be done to correct the problem.

Both of these ideas are, of course, untrue. To correct a tendency to catastrophize requires that a person must take control of the stream of his or her thought and avoid having dialogues of a catastrophic nature with himself or herself. He or she must stick with reality and avoid self-talk that runs on the order of "awful, irreplaceable, and disastrous." It is better to see life's accidents for what most of them really are—"unfortunate" but "correctable."

(2) *Overgeneralizing*. Closely allied to a tendency to catastrophize is the tendency to overgeneralize. One bad experience sets us up to expect another. A minister may preach poorly one Sunday and thereafter

expect to preach badly every Sunday, thus increasing his anxiety about preaching in general.

Overgeneralizing rapidly produces a negative and defeatist way of thinking. We come to expect that nothing will work for us. We deduce from a few setbacks that all our plans and goals are going to fail. This then becomes a self-fulfilling prophecy; what we fear may actually come about.

It is illogical thinking that causes overgeneralizing. Rejection, defeat, and failure in fulfilling one's expectations must be carefully evaluated to find the *real* cause of the failure. Rather than simply accepting a negative event as a defeat, we should analyze it and determine, as best we can, what went wrong. Then we can set about either correcting the error or avoiding a repeat of the failure.

(3) *Mislabeling*. It is remarkable how often we label an event incorrectly, and then react as if the label were correct. By placing an emotionally loaded label on an event we determine the course of our emotions.

A close friend of my wife recently became depressed over an encounter between them. My wife had innocuously canceled a luncheon engagement with this friend, who then interpreted the cancellation as personal rejection. She thought my wife was deliberately avoiding the friendship. She labeled the incident as "a sign that the friendship was over" and, having labeled it this way, naturally became upset and very depressed. When my wife realized how her action had been mislabeled, she quickly corrected the misunderstanding and restored the friendship.

A pastor can engage in mislabeling in many ways. When a project fails or a program he has designed doesn't work out, he may say, "I am a failure." Labeling himself as a failure may then trigger a depression appropriate to this belief.

When someone offers you advice, how often do we mislabel this as "criticism" and become depressed? Wouldn't it be better to force ourselves to label the advice correctly, accept it, realize we are not perfect, and thus avoid an unpleasant reaction? With a little attention to how we mislabel events, much depression can be avoided. When we discover that we are mislabeling, the thing to do is to correct the label with a more accurate one. The act of doing this can restore our emotional balance.

(4) *Overidentifying*. Overidentifying is a thinking style that causes us to be too dependent for our happiness on the happiness of others. We allow the moods of others to determine our moods.

Just recently, a pastor said to me "Every time my teenage son shows any sign of unhappiness, I feel terrible." He was overidentifying with his son. He became depressed whenever his son was depressed! This is common not only between parents and children, but also between spouses. Obviously, if the moods of others dictate our moods, we are going to be very moody!

Ministers' wives frequently find themselves overidentifying with their husbands. When he is down, she feels down. "I can tell from the look on his face when he walks in the front door whether I'm going to feel miserable all evening or not," one minister's wife told me. And this is also true for some husbands of women who are ministers.

One reason for this problem is that we tend to respond to each other with too much sympathy. We believe we owe each other the comfort of sympathetic suffering.

The clinical difference between sympathy and empathy is an important one for us to grasp. It has been shown again and again that it is empathy that provides comfort, healing, and help—*not* what is commonly understood to be sympathy. When a husband is depressed, he does not want his spouse to be depressed also (too many people believe this is sympathy), but rather he wants her to accept his feelings and understand his depression (this is true empathy).

The best way to "weep" with another and "bear" their burdens is to be *empathetic*. While becoming emotionally upset or sad through being associated with the pain of a loved one may sometimes be unavoidable, it is unnecessary and unhelpful to allow our emotions to follow too closely the ups and downs of others.

What is the solution? Simply to stop allowing others to control our moods. It is important to be understanding and to show compassion, but freeing ourselves from the need to feel what our wives, husbands, children, parents, or church members are feeling does not mean we don't love them or care about them. True empathy cares very deeply. But it realizes that truly *understanding* how others feel and *communicating this understanding* to them is what comforts and heals.

## Clarifying Values

All loss is related to values. We perceive as loss only the loss of those things which have value to us. To clarify and modify our values is, therefore, an important step in building resistance to depression.

It is easy for even intelligent and thoughtful people not to have a clear understanding of their values. In my opinion, one cannot follow the claims of Christ without giving careful attention to them, since so much of the gospel is a process of values clarification for an otherwise value-confused world.

What is a value? It may be defined as "the worth ascribed to a class of ideas or objects." We mostly attach worth to people, possessions, power, and privileges. In fact, we place value on everything that happens to or surrounds us based on our deep feelings about these things. There is nothing wrong with this tendency; it is a part of the way we are made and we cannot be totally free of it. Unfortunately, however, the deep feelings that underlie our values can sometimes be based on irrational ideas that are never put to the test of experience. For this reason we often develop misplaced or exaggerated values, and these can cause us unnecessary depression.

An example of such exaggerated values is our tendency to overvalue the opinions of others. We tailor our actions and opinions to be acceptable to the people around us, and we tend to become depressed whenever we experience disapproval from our peers. In our culture we also tend to overvalue possessions and money, power and prestige, work and ambition. And God has warned us against practically every one of these! Why? Because he has some arbitrary rules he wants us to keep? God never operates this way; this is how humans play games. No, God warns us against such exaggerated values for our own good; he knows how destructive they can be to us.

By understanding and developing our values, we build resistance to depression. Some values we hold may be destructive and need to be removed. Whatever else the process of sanctification is, it is, for me, a coming to terms with my values and a development of those values which God holds out to me as important for my spiritual and psychological well-being.

Nowhere is this issue of values more pertinent to our well-being than in our view of material things. To many individuals, the dollar is god (or so it seems from the way the loss of it triggers depression). Professional and social decisions are determined by how to get it, who has it, and what happens when you spend it. Holding too strong a value on material things can lead to tension, neurosis, and even emotional destruction. While I advocate that ministers must take an assertive stand on receiving fair wages for their labor, there is obviously a point at which "the love of money" becomes "the root of all evil," and God's Word clearly describes what our attitudes toward it must be.

Keeping close to God in our daily walk must surely influence our values, and hence decrease our susceptibility to depression. If we sense his protection, why should we be insecure? If we know his approval of our ministry, why should we need the approval of others? If we experience his grace and forgiveness, why should we fear failure?

I have found it useful in clarifying and modifying my own values to divide the world into two categories: essential things and nonessential things. Essential things are those things which have eternal significance, such as salvation and love. Nonessentials are those things I can touch and see—they become dust when it is all over. I pray for and work at increasing the value I attach to those things which are essential, and try to devalue the nonessentials, or at least to keep their value in the perspective of eternity. This helps me to stay sane!

## Avoiding Helplessness

I have already shown that feelings of helplessness can create depression. They represent a loss of control over one's environment and can trigger a state of passive inactivity. It is as if the individual does not believe he can do anything to control his or her environment and therefore stops trying.

The helplessness concept explains why many times, in the face of impending disaster, no steps are taken to avoid it. People simply give up.

While we are all capable of developing such feelings of helplessness, some of us are more prone to them than others. Helplessness becomes a personality style for some, who develop a predisposition to "give up" at the slightest hint of resistance. Sometimes this tendency is learned in childhood and is the product of an environment that was difficult to control or parents who exercised too much control. Whatever its origin, helplessness must be resisted; we must learn how to avoid helpless feelings if resistance to depression is to be built.

Underlying the reaction of helplessness is a faulty perception. The individual *perceives* that he or she cannot do anything to change circumstances and, believing this is true, retreats into nonactivity. Such a perception can cross over into many areas of life and can create a generalized perpetual helplessness.

What does God offer us to deal with helplessness? Paul seems to have found the answer in Philippians 4:13 when he says "I can do all things through Christ which strengtheneth me."

In addition to relying on the Lord's strength, it is important to understand that we can begin to alleviate the state of helplessness by the simple act of "taking control." Merely moving into *some* active mode, no matter how puny the effort may seem, can give one a feeling that control is being restored. This mobilizes the resources, both from God and from within ourselves, to deal with the crisis situation. No Christian needs to ever feel helpless, for we are given the promise that God "will never leave thee, nor forsake thee. So that we may boldly say, The Lord is my helper, and I will not fear what man shall do unto me" (Heb. 13:5–6).

# CONCLUSION

Ministers must constantly be growing—growing in self-understanding and in their experience of the power of God. The growth of the one fosters the experience of the other. The more we know about ourselves, the more we are able to tap the inexhaustible reservoirs of power that God provides. These reservoirs are open fully and freely to human hearts and minds, but if we do not know what our needs are, how can we intellectually draw on the supply for that need?

Ministers are always compelled to realize the limitations of their human frame. This is God's design. How else would people know that the power is from God and not from extraordinary pastors? Given this human limitation and the exacting demands of the ministry, the effective pastor will be the one who can match God's power to the awareness of his or her own needs.

I have, throughout this book, attempted to help the minister develop a greater understanding of himself or herself, the nature of his or her work, and the resources of God that are specifically designed to meet both the limitations of the minister's "earthen vessel" and the responsibilities of the ministry.

To implement this help I would strongly recommend that ministers develop a support group of other ministers and Christian workers as a means of sharing the encouragement and insight that will help them grow in self-understanding. Every pastor needs a pastor, and men and women of God have the same basic emotional needs as other men and women. In this sense Galatians 6:2 can have a special meaning for those called into the Lord's work: "Bear ye one another burdens, and so fulfill the law of Christ."

ARCHIBALD D. HART grew up in South Africa, where he first trained as a civil engineer. While working as a senior executive engineer, he did part-time counseling and lay preaching through his church. This experience convinced him his talents and calling lay in the area of Christian psychology, so at age 25 he went back to school to prepare for a second career in this field. After receiving his Ph.D. in clinical psychology from the University of Natal, he traveled to the U.S. to do a post-graduate fellowship at Fuller Theological Seminary's Graduate School of Psychology. He then returned to South Africa to set up a private practice, but shortly thereafter was invited to join the faculty at Fuller. He accepted and moved to California in 1973. In 1978 he became the first recipient of the Weyerhaeuser Award for Faculty Excellence and was appointed Associate Dean in 1979. He served as Associate Dean until 1982, when he became Acting Dean. He has been Dean of the Graduate School of Psychology at Fuller since 1983.

Dr. Hart specializes in psychotherapy from a Christian orientation, stress management, biofeedback techniques, neuropsychodiagnosis, and cognitive approaches to psychology. His major research interest is the vocational hazards of the ministry, and he has published several books, articles, and tapes on the subject, in addition to conducting workshops and conferences for ministers and teaching a seminary course on "mental health and the minister." In addition, he is active in professional organizations (having served on the board of the California State Psychological Association and as president of the California Biofeedback Society, of which he was a founding member); maintains an active private practice (seeing many ministers and their families as well as other Christian clients); and continues a prolific publishing career (numerous journal and magazine articles in addition to 4 other books: *Feeling Free; Depression: Coping and Caring; Children and Divorce: What to Expect, How to Help* and *The Success Factor: Discovering God's Potential through Reality Thinking).*

Dr. Hart's hobbies include sailing and electronics (he likes to build computers). He and his wife, Kathleen, live in Arcadia, California. They have three grown daughters: Catherine, Sharon, and Sylvia.